THE FOLKLORE SOCIETY

MISTLETOE SERIES

Symbols of Power

SYMBOLS OF POWER

edited by H.R.Ellis Davidson

Published by D.S.Brewer Ltd
and Rowman and Littlefield
for the Folklore Society
1977

Papers (c) 1973 by individual contributors

Published by D.S.Brewer Ltd.
240 Hills Road Cambridge
and P.O.Box 24 Ipswich IP1 1JJ

ISBN 0 85991 023 7

First published in the U.S.A. 1977 by
Rowman and Littlefield Totowa N.J.

Library of Congress Cataloging in Publication Data
Main entry under title:

Symbols of power,

    (Mistletoe series)
    Papers...given at a joint conference held by
the Folklore Society and the Department of
Religious Studies in the University of Lancaster
in 1973.
    1. Symbolism - Congresses. I. Davidson, Hilda
Roderick Ellis. II. Folk-lore Society, London.
III. Lancaster, Eng. University. Dept. of
Religious Studies. IV. Series: Mistletoe books.
BL600.S95 1977   291.3'7   76-55325
ISBN 0-87471-945-3

Dramrite Printers Ltd. London SE1

CONTENTS

List of Illustrations

PREFACE

THE PAPERS COLLECTED in this book were given at the conference held jointly by the Folklore Society and the Department of Religious Studies in the University of Lancaster in April 1973. This is the second of the inter-disciplinary conferences initiated by the Society; the first, on the Journey to the Other World, was published as a Mistletoe Book in 1975. We are most grateful to the University of Lancaster for the warm welcome which we received, to Professor Ninian Smart for giving the conference his blessing, and to Dr Eric Sharpe and Mrs Sharpe, who worked so hard to ensure that those who took part had a stimulating and enjoyable time.

The theme chosen was a wide one; this was deliberate, in order to throw light on different facets of the subject, and to open the way for further progress by bringing in contributions from a number of different disciplines. We chose to consider symbols not of authority but of spiritual and magical power, that energy which men have felt to be derived from a source beyond the familiar world. Folklore, which continually works through signs and symbols, must necessarily be involved in such a study, but to understand the search for symbols which has gone on from the earliest times of which men have left record, it is necessary to have some knowledge of the history of religious thought and imagery. Conversely, because of the characteristic simplicity and directness in popular protective and luck-bringing symbols, folklore may help to clarify man's choice of images to satisfy his deep instincts and the needs of his community. As Saxl put it in the opening essay in his book, *A Heritage of Images*:

The study of the history of images is one of the main problems common to all students of the humanities. Yet in our ordinary university teach-

ing it is of very little concern to us, and we
have little or no opportunity to talk about its
general features.

The major importance of the subject is indicated in the paper by Raymond Allchin on Religious
Symbols and Indian Thought, since he begins with
the claim by Paul Tillich that the object of
theology is the study of religious symbols, and
shows how this is supported by Indian teaching,
recognising as it does that God is formless and
nameless, and is only accessible to man through
symbols. In his paper and that of Michael Loewe,
on the strange and elaborate imagery on the silk
painting from a Chinese tomb of the second century
B.C., depicting the journey of a dead countess to
the Other World, we are reminded of the religious
aspect of the symbol, which may be either verbal
or visual. Again, in the paper by Eric Sharpe on
the Anglo-Saxon Runic Paternoster, and in that by
Venetia Newall on Icons, we find the symbols of
words and visual images placed side by side, and
are shown the different levels on which both can
operate. As man reaches out for protection in his
passage through a dark and menacing world, he
clutches instinctively at certain symbols, as a
magic means to ward off danger and misfortune, to
heal sickness, and to attain his immediate desires.
At a higher level, he can use the same symbols to
win through to new wisdom and understanding, and a
perception of meaning behind the confusion of life.
It is characteristic of symbols, as Tillich defined them, that they are continually changing in
significance, and in Kathleen Basford's paper on
the Green Man we have a detailed study of one
changing symbol, whose history she traces from the
late classical period to the English Middle Ages,
freeing us from some of the misconceptions which
arose from narrower interpretations of the arrest-
ing motif of the face surrounded by leaves.
Another illuminating example of a changing symbol

is given in Dr Allchin's account of varying representations of the Linga in Indian religious art,
for, contrary to Freudian theory, it did not begin
as a phallic symbol, nor is this its basic significance. In the last two papers, that by Katharine
Briggs on Symbols in Fairy Tales, and that by
Christina Hole on Protective Symbols in the Home,
we have two studies of the instinctive use of the
symbol in popular tales of magic and enchantment
on the one hand, and in attempts to keep away all
that threatens the safety of a household on the
other. While it was once thought that this kind of
folklore was a survival of earlier, more elaborate
religious beliefs in a pre-Christian period, it is
now recognised that certain symbols are continually reborn, changing their significance according
to the current needs of society, or the inspi-
ration of the artist who makes use of them.
Tillich claimed that symbols cannot be deliber-
ately produced; it is as if they possess an
obstinate life of their own, and as they die out
in one form they re-emerge in another. This life
moreover is a complex one; because they are
capable of more than one meaning, they are accepted by men in widely different periods of history
and put to manifold uses. Like the Green Man, the
most effective symbols can excite an imaginative
response in artist or story-teller, and to quote
Saxl again, they 'attract other ideas into their
sphere.' While such powerful symbols, like the
Linga, or the figures on the Icons, may become an
essential part of accepted religious teaching,
they may also remain part of the inherited tradition of simple people, giving expression to what
would be impossible for them to put into words.
Such symbols may be apprehended through the eyes,
or the ears, or by sharing in corporate action.
Examples of the last are the symbolism behind the
funeral rites of the nobles of the Han dynasty in
China, and the rites in which icons play a major

part, while we were reminded of other examples by
films shown by members of the Society at the conference, which depicted such ceremonies as the
raising of a maypole and the lighting of bonfires.

At the lively discussion held at the close, we
were all conscious of a desire to follow up the
many problems raised by the work on symbols which
is presented here. Throughout the centuries
schools of thought have resented and distrusted
symbols as dangerous and superstitious; we have
the iconoclasts of Byzantium who destroyed the
icons, the Puritans of the seventeenth century who
disfigured the images and prohibited the Maypole
and Christmas celebrations, the Soviet opposition
to the symbols of the Russian Orthodox Church. Do
beliefs which are obviously superstitious weaken
the power of symbols? At what stage do old symbols
become truly outworn, and need to die, and do
those who seek to banish symbols of power inevi-
tably replace them by new symbols in a different
form, or by the old disguised as something new? We
had little opportunity to discuss the use of
symbols of power for evil ends, or to reach any
conclusions as to the most profitable means of
defining symbols, and the best methods of study.
But it is hoped that this group of papers may
demonstrate the way in which interdisciplinary
studies of this kind may contribute to a fuller
understanding of a subject in which many of us are
interested, but which in these days of specialis-
ation we tend to consider from one standpoint
alone.

H.R.ELLIS DAVIDSON

1. RELIGIOUS SYMBOLS AND INDIAN THOUGHT

F.R.Allchin

THE CONCEPT OF the religious symbol occupies an
important place in the systematic theology of Paul
Tillich. It appears to have a long and interesting
history, bearing a major resemblance to the
analogia entis of St.Thomas, which in its turn represents a resolution of the literalist and alle-
gorist hermeneutic orientations which at least
since the time of Origen had formed rival schools
of scriptural interpretation. The aim of the
present paper is to examine how far Tillich's concept may usefully be applied to Indian religious
terms and whether there appears to emerge a
history of Indian religious symbols as a result.
It is not my intention to consider the weighty
philosophic questions raised by Tillich's religious symbols; nor is it my intention to examine
the indigenous Indian concepts of symbols and indigenous hermeneutic orientations, interesting as
these must be. To do so is certainly beyond the
scope of this paper, and although it will be
necessary to touch on the Indian traditional
interpretations, we shall do so primarily from the
outside, leaving aside for another occasion the
inner questions, which require more extensive and
somewhat different treatment. At the same time,
the application of Tillich's usage appears so
meaningful in the Indian context, that we are left
in no doubt that somewhat similar ideas must in
early times have been current there also.

Many references to the religious symbol are to
be found in Tillich's writings.[1] Here, I shall
introduce a synthesis of these references, treat-
ing the usage as being more or less consistent
throughout. He states that the direct object of
theology is not God, but, rather, the religious
symbol.[2] In these symbols is expressed that which

1

is the content of every religion, the basis of
every religious experience and the foundation of
every theology, the divine-human encounter. These
things involve man's visions of ultimate concern,
and hence man's ultimate concern must be expressed
symbolically. Symbols have several characteristic
features. The first is that they point beyond
themselves to something else. Signs also point
beyond themselves, but they differ from symbols in
that there is no intrinsic relationship between
the sign and the thing indicated, whereas the
symbol 'actually participates in the power of that
which it symbolizes'. Therefore signs can be replaced for reasons of expedience or convention,
while symbols cannot. This participation is the
second characteristic of the symbol. The flag, for
example, participates in the power and dignity of
the nation for which it stands. But this is not so
with the mere sign. The third characteristic is
that a symbol opens up levels of reality, of meaning and of being, which would otherwise be closed
to us. Tillich cites the example of works of art
in this connection. The fourth characteristic is
that a symbol also opens up corresponding dimensions and elements of meaning and reality in the
human mind. We cannot become aware of such dimensions except through symbols. Symbols cannot be
produced intentionally — this is the fifth characteristic. They grow out of the individual or
collective unconscious, and cannot function without being accepted by the unconscious dimension of
our being. And the sixth and last characteristic
of the symbol is that, like a living thing, it
grows and dies, according to the way in which it
produces response in people.

What is true of symbols in general is also true
of the religious symbol. This has a special
character in that it points towards the ultimate
level of being, to ultimate reality, to being
itself. Hence it participates in the power of the

2

ultimate to which it points. Religious symbols are
neither produced by theology, nor destroyed by it.
They are the products of the encounter of God and
man. Nevertheless, they too have a life of their
own, are born and die. This means that when the
form of encounter which produced them disappears,
they may lose their validity, become debased, and
lose their original symbolic content.

Tillich also refers to a 'typology' of religious symbols.[3] He sees them as operating on
several levels. The higher levels he calls Transcendent symbols, being those which point to the
'holy' itself. These include at the basic level
symbols pointing towards God; then symbols pointing to His attributes and His actions (creating,
helping, etc.). Symbols on the lower level he
calls Immanent. These are those which refer to the
appearance of the holy in space and time. Among
these there are also several levels. First, are
incarnations, then sacramental symbols, and third,
at the largely liturgical level, sign-symbols.
This last group constitutes a vast realm of signs
which may from time to time be elevated to pos-
itions of power. Tillich also speaks in one place
of the critical appraisal of symbols, as being one
of the roles of theology, so as to prevent their
reduction to non-symbolic thinking, with conse-
quent loss of meaning and power, and hence guard
against their degeneration to mere idolatrous
signs.

Finally Tillich develops his theory of the
religious function of symbols, to include also
myths. I regret that this interesting aspect of
the subject must for the present paper be left
aside.

In order to provide a framework of ideas within
which we may consider the working of religious
symbols in the Indian context, we cannot do better
than look at a passage from the Śatapatha Brāhmaṇa,
which forms one of the many creation stories of

3

the Late Vedic and Brāhmaṇa periods.[4] This tells
that in the beginning 'that (that is to say, this
universe) was Brahman' (n.). It created the *devas*,
gods, and it made them ascend their respective
worlds (*loka*). Agni, fire, ascended this world;
Vayu, wind, the aerial regions; and Sūrya, sun,
the heavens. The gods who were above these it made
ascend the worlds above these; and just as these
three are manifest in their worlds, so are those
gods too manifest in their worlds. Then Brahman
itself went up to the sphere beyond. And reaching
there it thought, 'How can I descend again into
these worlds?' It descended again by means of
these two, Name and Form, ...and as far as there
are Name and Form, so far extends this (creation).
These are the two great powers of Brahman, and
verily he who knows these two great powers of
Brahman himself becomes a great power. These are
indeed the two great manifestations (*yakṣa*) of
Brahman, and he who knows them becomes himself a
great manifestation. One of these two is greater,
namely Form, for what is Name is also Form. As if
in amplification of this story the Brihadāraṇyaka
Upaniṣad[5] speaks of the universe as a triad of
Names, Forms and Works; and speaks of Voice or
Speech (*vāc*) as the Brahman of Names, the Eye as
the Brahman of Forms, and the Self as the Brahman
of Works. These three are together a unity consti-
tuting the immortal (*amṛita*) hidden by (or in) the
real (*satya*).

These passages are of great interest because
they tell us in mythological guise several important things. The first names Brahman (n.) as the
creator of all 'this' universe. It refers to the
subsequent and lesser creation of the Vedic gods
and their being assigned to their respective
spheres. When Brahman had ascended to a realm
beyond, he created Names and Forms as a means of
again descending into them, and maintaining a link
with his creatures. Name and Form are described as

4

the powers or manifestations (*yakṣa*) of Brahman,
and who knows them becomes a power or manifestation. Without wishing to touch on the difficulty
of translating Brahman or Yakṣa in these passages,
I think we may conclude that viewed from the standpoint of man as one of the creatures, Name and
Form occupy an intermediary role which may best be
described as symbolic, pointing to the ultimate
reality which lies 'beyond', and participating in
its power.

This association of Name and Form as attributes
of created things is as old as the Vedas, but it
continued for long to occupy a place in Indian
thought. To illustrate the sort of continuity we
are thinking of we shall cite a single passage,
some twenty centuries later than the Brāhmaṇa we
have just quoted, but surely relevant in our context. The passage comes from the opening sections
of the Rāmacaritamānasa of Tulsīdās. Tulsī begins
with his statement of what may be called the
central paradox of Indian theology. This is
immediately followed by a credal statement of
great significance, emphasising the unity of God,
who is formless and nameless, who is all-pervasive
and *saccidānanda*; who for the sake of his devotees
assumed a human body and did many deeds, etc.[6]
Then follows a group of reverential verses addressed to various persons, culminating in Rām.
This leads Tulsī to a long passage extolling the
wonder, beauty, power and virtue of the name of
Rām.[7] In the course of this he returns to the
theme he has already introduced. The Name, he says,
and the object named are to one another as master
and servant. Name and Form are both attributes
(*upādhi*) of the Lord, unspeakable and without
beginning, but understandable to right intelligence. The mystery of the Name is an untold (or
perhaps untellable) story, comforting to understand, but which may not be described. The Name is
a good witness between both the Saguṇa and Nirguṇa

aspects of God, a wise interpreter revealing both (to man).[8] There are these two aspects of God, both are unspeakable, unfathomable, without beginning. 'To my mind', says Tulsī, 'the Name is greater than either aspect, in that it has established command over both by its powers. Both aspects of God are (by themselves) inaccessible (to man), but they are of easy access through the Name. Therefore do I say that the Name is greater both than Brahman (the Nirguṇa aspect) and Rām (the Saguṇa)'.[9]

Here then we see a similar role for the Name and Form, as good witnesses, attributes of the nameless and formless deity, making it accessible to man. These two passages provide us with a conceptual framework within which we may begin to understand the Indian religious symbols. They prompt us to remark that while all names and forms did not become religious symbols, all are potentially so; or to put it the other way round all religious symbols have been elevated from among objects having names and/or forms. We are now ready to consider some examples of the way in which names and forms have been thus elevated.

As we have seen both names and forms are available for elevation to the role of religious symbols. From the former come those symbols in which the verbal element predominates, from the latter come the primarily visual symbols. Many symbols of course combine both elements. There is in the literature a varying emphasis on the one aspect or the other. As we saw the Śatapatha Brāhmaṇa regarded the form as dominant, while Tulsīdās regarded the name as superior to the form. Throughout the history of Indian religions both verbal and visual symbols have arisen, flourished and fallen again into obscurity. The repertoire of Brāhmanical or Hindu symbols, is to a large extent shared, though differently used, by Buddhism and Jainism. It would be interesting to trace both the

6

broad history of this tendency and its main
periods. The Vedas, as our first written source,
are already preceded by the still 'prehistoric'
Indus civilization, from which certain visual
symbols are already evident, and these symbols
have a long subsequent history. Among them the
pīpal leaf and tree, the svastika, the snake and
perhaps also the linga are good examples. While
there is still much room for discussion of the
relationship between the Vedas themselves and
their traditional interpretation in the Late Vedic
and Brāhmaṇa periods, it is evident that a whole
range of major Vedic symbols was retained and
developed then, and that many of these, even if in
a somewhat obsolescent state, have survived in
Indian tradition from that time forward. The
period of the early Upaniṣads witnessed the rise
of a whole new series of concepts and symbols, and
this in its turn hastened the loss of meaning of
some of those of the Vedic period. In the same way
the period of the composition of the Mahābhārata
and the Bhagavadgītā, and the rise of sectarian
Vaiṣṇavism and Śaivism saw the emergence of a new
series of symbols, and so on. It would also be
interesting to trace the history of some of the
great symbols as they have developed and ramified
through the ages. Some of them could almost be
used to demonstrate the entire process. Thus for
example the wheel (cakra) had already grown from
being merely a chariot wheel to being the wheel of
existence and divine order (bhava cakra, ṛita
cakra) upon which all things are set, and hence
too the wheel of time, in the Rigveda.[10] The
Buddha chose the wheel as the symbol of the Dharma
(Dharma cakra), and the promulgation of his teaching was spoken of as the turning of the wheel of
the Dharma (Dharma cakra parivartana). This is the
wheel which enters the visual record with the
capitals of Asokan columns in the third century
B.C.; and which more than two thousand years later

was chosen as the symbol of independent India. The
same wheel, in the form of a discus, became one of
the great emblems of Viṣṇu and enjoyed its own
rich development as a symbol both verbal and
visual.[11]

We now wish to consider a selected number of
symbols, drawn somewhat arbitrarily, but widely,
from Indian religious texts and examine them in
greater detail, considering at the same time how
far they conform to the characteristics of the
religious symbol as they were set out by Tillich.
We shall attempt to move forward in time, starting
with those which had reached their full development at the earliest period, and going on to those
whose later development seems more important for
our theme.

The Rigveda supplies a rich body of material
for our analysis. Among the deities of the Veda is
one Vāc, sacred utterance. Vāc is a feminine noun
meaning speech, originally no more and no less.
But in the Veda it becomes elevated to a special
sacred meaning as Vedic utterance or holy speech.
It comes to be conceived as a divine being, as a
'personification of Vedic hymnal composition'.[12]
It comes to be regarded as something peculiarly
holy, manifesting the divine. Indeed it comes to
have a connotation not far removed from the word
śruti, and therefore comparable to the word
Revelation. In the Rigveda we are told that many,
though seeing, do not see this holy speech, many,
though hearing, do not hear it, yet to others she
has revealed herself, like a fair clothed bride,
willingly to her husband.[13] In another context
Speech speaks as a queen, who 'bears all the gods,
extends through all the worlds, even to heaven,
even beyond (para) heaven and earth'.[14] Thus
Speech becomes one of the goddesses of the Rigveda.
Here then we see something which is very close to
Tillich's religious symbol. Common speech is
available to all, but in certain contexts, and for

8

certain persons, common speech becomes sacred
Speech, and as such she points far beyond herself,
bearing all the other gods, extending through all
the worlds, to heaven and to what is beyond. We
are reminded here of the cosmology implied by the
Śatapatha Brāhmaṇa passage we quoted above. The
Creator (here *brahman*, n.) created the different
orders, set the gods in their various heavenly
stations and then retired 'beyond'. This 'beyond'
has here and elsewhere a clear sense of ultimacy,
and thus the religious symbol of sacred Speech has
a role pointing towards the ultimate. We have no
doubt that these mighty Vedic utterances, en-
compassed by Speech, participate in the power towards which they point; nor that Speech (*Vāc*) can
open up for us levels of meaning and reality which
would otherwise be closed to us. Thus it fulfils
the second and third of Tillich's criteria. That
in so doing it opens up comparable new dimensions
of our own minds is equally certain. This after
all is the role of Revelation, and of the Vedic
hymns as revealed texts. We cannot say whether it
fulfils the fifth characteristic, that of the
symbol not being the production of intention, but
this seems a very plausible inference. That Speech
as a goddess loses something of her prime role in
later periods, although surviving and still living
as an element of the living Vedic tradition,
surely justifies the sixth characteristic. Thus
Vāc, Speech, has become a religious symbol, symbolising Revelation as it is 'heard' by the Riṣis,
pointing towards ultimate reality, towards things
of ultimate concern. We may note in passing that
Brahman has among its earliest Vedic meanings a
comparable usage of holy word, word of power. We
may also test our conclusions by considering three
more references to Vāc from the long and enigmatic
Asya Vāmasya hymn.[15] In the first verse four
riddles are proposed and in the second answered.
We shall mention two of them below (in connection

9

with sacrifice). The one we are here concerned
with asks of the highest abode of Speech, and
answers that Brahman is the highest abode of
speech. Thus in the verse the deified utterance
finds her highest abode in the ultimate, in
Brahman. The third verse tells us that speech is
divided into four quarters, three are concealed in
a cave, and one men speak. The speech of men is
the observable part of a higher phenomenon, and
the intrinsic connection of common speech to
higher, and highest, things emphasises its role as
a symbol of power.

Another example of a Vedic deity which seems to
illustrate the same process of the rise of a religious symbol is fire, Agni. In spite of the very
widespread reverence for fire in ancient times, as
a magical or supernatural potency, it occupies in
the Veda a peculiarly major position, second only
to Indra. Common fire as we see it on earth is already full of potency, but when the fire is
kindled in accordance with ritualistic injunctions
in the fire altar, and receives the offerings cast
into it by the sacrificial priest, it becomes at
once Agni the god, who serves as the messenger of
the gods, carrying men's offerings up to heaven,
and bringing back the other gods to participate in
the sacrifice. From the many references to Agni in
the Rigveda we need only quote from one hymn to
reveal the whole process.[16] The very first hymn of
the first book of the Rigveda is addressed to Agni.
'I praise Fire, who is the *purohita* priest, the
god of the sacrifice, the *ritvij* priest, the *hotā*
priest,[1]...he shall bring hither the gods[2]...
The perfect sacrifice which Fire encompasses goes
truly to the gods[4]...May Fire, the wise priest,
the god, bring hither the gods.[5]' Thus common
fire becomes sacred Fire, becomes a god, the
heaven-sent messenger of the gods. Finally in
verse 8 of the same hymn he becomes the protector
of the universal order (*gopāmṛtasya*) a mysterious

term, but one which is suggestive of man's views
of ultimate concern. In this way fire, as fully as
speech, reveals all the characteristics of a religious symbol, bound up with the whole mysterious
sacrifical ritual around which Vedic religion re-
volved.

The symbolism of the Sun in the Vedas and
indeed in the later Vedic period is extraordi-
narily rich and relevant for our purpose. The Sun
becomes identified with several deities, each representing special aspects, Pūṣan the nourishing
aspect, Savitri the stimulative, Sūrya, Āditya,
Varuṇa, etc. Just as Agni, Fire, is the ruling
deity on the earthly sphere, so is Sūrya, Sun, on
the heavenly. Indeed there is a direct relationship, analogical or homological, between the two.
The significance of the symbolism of the sun is
greatly enhanced by the many references to it in
the Brāhmaṇas and early Upaniṣads. I have discussed this symbolism in greater detail elsewhere,
and I do not wish to repeat it here.[17] But I may
briefly summarise the main conclusions. The
physical sun is elevated to the role of a deity,
or rather a number of deities; but at the same
time he is repeatedly seen in terms of the ultimate. In one place in the Rigveda Sūrya is referred to as the *ātman* of (all) moving and unmoving
(things).[18] More significantly he is referred to
as the 'bird' (*suparṇa*) or shining bird who is
really one, but who is spoken of by the wise as
many.[19] The references to 'the one' seem to provide a basis for a sort of nascent monotheistic
symbolism. In a passage in the Yajurveda, the sun
is described by the words, 'The face of truth is
covered by a golden disc'.[20] This disc is literally a disc worn during initiation, but symbolically it is the sun. The sun itself however is but
another symbol masking the brilliance of the
hidden face of truth. Here then there is no naive
identification of the sun with ultimate truth, nor

of Savitri with the sun. Both are covers masking
the reality to which they point, and sharing in
its power. The longevity of the Gāyatrī prayer and
its universality, indicate the response of power
which the sun opens up in the human mind, and
therefore stand witness to one of the oldest and
most enduring symbols in Indian religion.

We have selected these examples because they
are reasonably clear and unequivocal, and because
their full development appears already to have
taken place during the Vedic period. Many other
examples could have been selected. There are
others, however, which even if their initial elevation seems to have started during the Vedic
period, or is partly attested in the Vedic
Saṃhitās, only reached their full development or
significance as symbols in the subsequent, late
Vedic or early Upaniṣadic periods. We notice among
these the new emphases which developed then, even
if there appears to have been an unbroken tradition of interpretation linking the two periods.
Among these symbols some are extremely difficult
to trace. Such a one is *Brahman*, whose Vedic
origins still leave room for controversy, although
the Upaniṣadic usage is reasonably well established. Another symbol of this sort is *Ātman*;
another *prāṇa* which begins with the simple meaning
of breath and comes to assume a meaning rather
closer to life-spirit. But of all the symbols of
this group perhaps the most remarkable is *Oṃ*. Oṃ
is used as an opening of all recitations of the
Vedas. Although it does not occur in the text of
either the Rigveda or Atharvaveda, its use must
be as old as the compilation of the Saṃhitās. It
occurs perhaps for the first time in the Yajurveda, where it is known as *praṇava*, reverberant;
while in the context of the Sāmaveda it is known
as *udgītha*. Thus both these early contexts empha-
sise the sung or sounded aspect. In the Upaniṣads
we find a quite remarkable development. The

12

Kaṭhopaniṣad refers to Oṃ as that word which all
the Vedas record... That imperishable word is (or
means) Brahman, that syllable means the highest.[21]
The Taittirīya Upaniṣad states that Oṃ is Brahman,
Oṃ is this whole universe.[22] The place thus
reached by the syllable Oṃ has never been lost.
Thus Kṛiṣṇa in the Bhagavadgītā, in a passage describing the way he is present in different
categories of things, states 'I am the praṇava in
all the Vedas',[23] and in another place speaks of
Oṃ as ekākṣaraṃ brahma, God in one syllable.[24] In
modern times Svāmī Dayānanda has called Oṃ 'the
supreme name of God'.[25] Thus Oṃ offers a remarkable symbol. Apart from the three phonemic
elements, and its context as a reverberant sound
opening and ending Vedic recitations, it has no
clear connotation at the literal level. And yet it
came to point as a symbol towards Brahman, the
absolute of the Upaniṣads, and to encompass 'all
this' created universe. Viewed as a religious
symbol it is one of the most ancient, widely dif-
fused and universal in all Indian tradition, com-
bining in later periods when writing became common
a special written form with its sounded aspect.
   The latest of the early group of Upaniṣads, for
example the Śvetāśvatara, show a marked change in
language and style. The old intuitive symbols of
the earlier periods are being replaced by a new
and more intellectually controlled group of terms.
Yet among these some of the new symbols which were
to dominate the thought of later centuries were
already arising. The same tendency is clearly
visible in the Bhagavadgītā. In these works the
new vision of God, either as Śiva or as Bhagavān,
Kṛiṣṇa or Viṣṇu, presents new symbols so powerful
that they swept into obscurity or neglect many of
the older perspectives and their symbols. Along
with the great symbols for God a whole new series
of sacramental symbols came into being. We can
trace the process at work in the modification of

13

older symbols such as *yajña*, sacrifice.

The richness and variety of meanings which an Indian religious symbol can achieve are well demonstrated by *yajña*. Sacrifice occupies a predominant sacramental role from the time of the Rigveda onwards. It is there intimately related to fire, Agni, the god of the sacrifice, and although this connection later loses much of its power, *yajña* remains in India the sacramental symbol par excellence. Already in the Vedas the seeds of later growth are present in embryonic form. Bergaigne has discussed the sacrifice in terms of the 'analogy' it presents between earthly things and heavenly phenomena.[26] This at once suggests the symbolic role of sacrifice. The main elements are the gift of the sacrificial goods to the fire (properly laid on the Vedic fire altar), so that Agni may convey them to the appropriate gods.[27] In return the god will be brought down to earth, and bestow rewarding gifts on men. When the sacrificial goods are not consumed by the fire, for instance in an animal sacrifice or sacrifice of food derived from products of the cow, they are ultimately consumed by the priests, sacrificer and others, being (as we shall see) what is later called *Prasāda*, grace. But as Bergaigne realised, the sacrificial symbol went far beyond this. The sacrifice provided already a kind of magic symbol by which the skilled priests might intervene in the world of the gods, the macrocosm, by the performance of the correct ritual acts in the world of men. Thus in one way the sacrifice had an intimate relationship to cosmic order, *rita*.

The microcosm-macrocosm symbolism is epitomised in the Puruṣa Sūkta which focusses a whole range of related ideas.[28] This hymn is from the latest stratum of the Rigveda, and may suggest the growth of ideas in later Vedic times. In the hymn the sacrifice of Puruṣa, macrocosmic man, by the gods is seen as the act of creation, and the analogy of

14

macrocosmic man to microcosmic man is linked to this concept, thus providing the cosmic analogy of sacrifice, and charging the sacramental terms with a new intensity of meaning. In this context the four riddles of the Asya Vāmasya hymn of the Rigveda, of which we cited one above, are particularly suggestive. 'I ask of the farthest limit of nature (Prithivi); of the navel of the world (Bhuvana); of the horse's strong seed; and of the highest abode of Speech (Vāc)'.[29] The answer is extraordinary; 'This sacrificial altar is the farthest bound of Nature; this sacrifice is the Navel of the world; Soma (the sacrificial potion) is the horse's strong seed; Brahman (or the Brahman priest) is the highest abode of Speech'. Here then the altar carries us to the farthest bounds of created nature; and the sacrifice brings us back to the mysterious Omphalos the centre and issuing point of creation. Space does not permit me to discuss the fourth great symbol of this passage, Soma. As is so often the case in the developing continuum of Indian civilization, we are left with the feeling that, in terms of all later developments, the meaning attached to some of the hymns during the late stage of Vedic composition, and during the stage of compilation of the completed Saṃhitā of the Rigveda, has acquired a profundity of which only the germ was there in the original composition.

The meaning of sacrifice develops in the succeeding centuries, so that now Keith can write of it as a 'piece of magic pure and simple'.[30] The theory of sacrifice, as we find it in the Brāhmaṇas, is virtually a new creation, although the germ is certainly present in the Rigveda. This is clear when we realise that the basis of the system is the identification of the sacrifice with the creator, Prajāpati. In their ramifications the accounts of creation are given a mythological basis, but are interpreted in terms of symbols.

15

The two levels of interpretation, the human, microcosmic, level and the macrocosmic, daimonic, level, run through the whole discussion of sacrifice. In this period the discussions of the sacrifices and their minutiae are multiplied ad nauseam, and in the process there is enormous scope for developing a host of sign-symbols in the mechanics of the ritual.

The theory of sacrifice and its symbolism crystalised in the age of the Brāhmaṇas and provides the basis for the tradition of Vedic sacrifices, often referred to as Karma Kāṇḍa, through the centuries and down to modern times. It has long been regarded as a sterile field, and as fossilised, by other branches of Hinduism, and distaste for it is expressed already in the later Upaniṣads.[31] The same theme is developed in the Bhagavadgītā,[32] and along with it the Gītā offers us a new and profoundly interesting symbolism of sacrifice. Sacrifice is now generalised, even universalised, and linked with acts, karma, which are likewise universalised. The Gītā remembers the association of the creator Prajāpati with Sacrifice,[33] and summarises the traditional sacrifice in these terms. It is ordained by the creator, in order to sustain the gods, so that they reciprocally may sustain man. The gods will give food, and those who eat the leavings of the sacrifice are freed from taint. All beings are born of food; food of rain; rain of sacrifice; and sacrifice from works (karma). Its own special doctrine of sacrifice is built on this foundation. The nature of Karma is profound and difficult to understand.[34] The true Karmayogī sees work in worklessness, in worklessness, work. He works for sacrifice alone. God is the offering, God the sacrifical butter, offered by God in God's fire. Any thing and any act can be done as a sacrifice, even sacrifice itself: the senses or their objects, wealth, penance, yoga, study and knowledge, food, even the

16

very act of breathing. 'So many and various are the sacrifices spread out athwart the mouth of Brahman. They spring from work, all of them'.[35] In this way, according to Ranade, the Gita reconciles the antinomy between Jñāna and Karma.

Here then in the Gītā, yajña, sacrifice, has become a sacramental symbol of remarkable depth and power, pointing towards God through work and hence through man in society. In terms of the Indian theology of man this marks a development of fundamental importance.

Other elements of the sacrifice, or associated with it, also played a role as symbols. Among them was *dakṣiṇa*, the fee paid by the sacrificer to the officiating priest. This word had clearly a symbolic role in the Rigveda,[36] but it seems to have lost its symbolic character at a very early date, and scarcely plays a role as a religious symbol thereafter. A striking contrast is provided by *prasāda*, which having originally the meaning of graciousness, kindness, early acquired a special connotation in terms of the food and other things offered to a god in the course of worship or sacrifice. This is either retained by the priest, or returned to the worshipper, or distributed by the priest to others. The distributed goods are referred to as Prasāda, and bring with them a portion of the special grace of the god to the recipient. From this usage the word, along with certain other terms, became a religious symbol, divine Grace, and came to play a major role in the theology of devotional Hinduism.[37]

But the demands of the growing popular stream of Bhakti, devotion, led to other interesting symbols, and I wish now to consider a group which arose in this context. The first is the religious teacher or preceptor, *ācārya* or *guru*, who since the beginning has occupied an important position in Indian tradition. When a boy is invested with the sacred thread and enters Brahmacarya Āśrama he

17

takes up residence in the house of a teacher who begins to instruct him in the Vedas, imparting spiritual wisdom. That there should have developed between teacher and pupil a special bond is understandable, and it is in this light that we may understand the words of the Taittirīya Upaniṣad.[38] 'Let your mother be a god to you; let your father be a god to you; let your teacher be a god to you; let your guest be a god to you'. Again, the special relationship is plain in many of the Vedic Śānti mantras, 'May that (Brahman) protect me, may that (Brahman) protect the teacher (vaktā)'.[39] At a later date the role of the teacher developed into something still more important. For the medieval devotees the teacher becomes a living symbol for God. Let us look at a few examples. In the Dohās of Kabīr there is a very graphic treatment of the subject. Many of his verses express the sort of respect which might be expected of a disciple: the glory of the true Guru (Satguru) is infinite, infinite assistance did he give me; he opened my eyes to the infinite, he showed me the infinite.[40] The true guru has taken his bow in hand and released his arrows; one which he shot with love has remained lodged in my body.[41] But in others we find a different emphasis. In a verse of somewhat doubtful authenticity he says, 'the Guru and Govind (God) both stand before me, to which should I approach? As I sacrifice myself, it is to you, O teacher, for you have shown me God'.[42] 'The Guru and Govind are one, only the form is different, if self is abolished and one living dies, then does he meet the Creator'.[43] 'I offer myself to the Guru, as I am a sacrifice!, for he has made a God from a mere man in no time at all'.[44] From these passages we find that the Guru and God are identified, that the Guru is even put before God in that he it is who can open our eyes to God, and that the Guru has the wonderful power of turning a mere man into God himself. This Guru is truly a

18

very wonderful symbol!

We find a similar line of thought in other saints. Jñānadeva's Amṛitānubhava opens with a eulogy of his Guru. The teacher's powers even sur-pass those of Śiva (God), he is like a mirror in which the self can see its bliss.[45] Though mani-fest he is invisible; though he is light, he does not illuminate. He exists, yet he is nowhere.[46] He is indescribable in words, for they become silent in the face of his oneness which tolerates no duality.[47] When one tries to bow to him he does not remain before one as the object of reverence.[48] The words master and disciple mean but one reality and the master alone lives in both forms.[49] Here too, the disciple finds in the teacher the absol-ute unity which indicates that the teacher is none other than God. In Nānak and the Sikh Gurus this tendency continues with even greater clarity. The true teacher (Satguru) is God and God only, in-effable and indescribable.[50] Do not believe that he is the form of a man. In this development we become aware of an interesting situation, which the character of the symbol produces: either the Guru is identified with God, or God is identified with the Guru. We may recall Tulsī's somewhat similar discussion of the theme of the divine Name (see above, p.5) which is even to be preferred to God, because without it (as a symbol) God is in-accessible.

The Vīraśaiva literature reveals a closely com-parable attitude towards the Guru, and his re-lationship with the disciple. In Śūnyasampādane we learn that Allama Prabhu exemplified the Śivād-vaita doctrine that the disciple is himself the master, and that the experience of God burned in him like the feeling of fire becoming camphor, even before his own intuition had led him into the secret chamber where his Guru to be, Animiṣadeva, sat in trance.[51] Once there the sight alone of the glorious Guru brought for him instantaneous en-

lightenment, and therefore here too the sight of
the Guru coincided with the vision of God. Allama
realised that as the teacher was quite oblivious
(being in profound trance) he must seek his own
initiation from himself as Guru.[52] He realised
that the Guru is no less than the undifferentiated
image of his own heart, and so he took the Linga
resting on the Guru's palm. At that very moment
the Guru passed into the Absolute Void.[53] Allama
in the ensuing moments dispelled his natural grief
with the realisation that he was now one with the
Guru, and no less one with the ultimate.[54] It
would require more space than I have today to
develop this subject as it deserves, or to consider the inherent dangers of the debasement of
the symbol. Who for example can arbitrate between
a false Guru and the true Guru? and how would such
discrimination operate in practice? How far and in
what way does divine Grace come in? But I hope
that these examples will serve to show the way in
which the Guru becomes a symbol in every sense of
the word.

I now wish to pass on to a symbol of considerable importance, and one which has a long history,
this is the company of saints or spiritual community (sādhusanga, satsanga). Although there must
have been such gatherings from ancient times and
the early Upaniṣads provide many instances of religious gatherings, and although there is good
evidence that the related Buddhist term Sangha
early assumed importance as a Buddhist religious
symbol, yet the term in question only emerges with
symbolic content for Hinduism in later times,
probably in the first millennium A.D. As the
symbol shows elements which are held in common by
the Christian 'oikonomia' it is interesting to
consider the somewhat parallel development of the
two. The importance of association with holy
people is clearly anticipated in the Bhagavadgītā
when the service of the wise is extolled,[55] or

when the mutual enlightenment of the devotees
while they are engaged in telling the divine story
is mentioned.[56] As a natural concomitant of the
growing streams of Vaiṣṇava and Śaiva devotion the
communal aspects of worship and service find expression in their literature, and it was probably
thus that the symbol rose to importance. It is
somewhat surprising to me when I look back to my
own early contacts with Indian religion, or to my
subsequent reading of mainly European (but also
Indian) writers on the subject, to recall how
little reference there was to Satsanga. I only
gradually became aware of it at a later date, when
I again and again encountered powerful expressions
of regard in the saints of the past ten centuries.

In the Indian context the spiritual community
exists at several different levels. At base it is
a group of like-minded people who gather together,
often around a Guru or some such personality, for
regular meetings which may involve hymn singing,
devotional practices, repetitions of the divine
Name or Names, readings and expositions of the
scriptures, or meditation. The meetings of such a
group constitute a Satsanga and the group assumes
an entity of its own. The term should not strictly
be used for the wider membership of a sect, and in
this way it differs from the older and more
clearly organised Buddhist Sangha, which is more
nearly analogous to the Christian church; but it
is occasionally used in this wider sense, and in
so far as any meeting of the members of such a
sect is likely to develop into a Satsanga, the
usage is a logical extension. As the word assumed
importance, its symbolic content increased, and
sometimes it came to mean the whole body of
believers who feared God, and in some respects may
be compared to the Christian concept of the Kingdom of God.

In commenting on Bhagavadgītā x.9 Jñānadeva
speaks of the overflowing of joy in the soul com-

municating with others. While the Guru gives his
teaching in secret and solitude, those devotees
who associate with each other proclaim the message
to all in a thundrous voice; and in his comment on
iv.34 he calls the service of the feet of saints
the very threshold to the temple of knowledge.[57]
In Vinayapatrikā Tulsīdās describes the spiritual
community as the very limbs of God and as the
essence that emerges from the churning of the
milky ocean of the Vedas.[58] He prays that wherever
he may take birth, in whatever womb or form, he
may have devotion to God and communion with others
who share his devotion. In Rāmacaritamānasa he
gives an extended metaphor of Satsanga as a mobile
king of pilgrim resorts (that is to say Prayāg),
in which devotion is the Ganges, desire for God
the Sarasvatī, sermons are the Jamunā, and stories
of Viṣṇu and Śiva are the Sangam (confluence of
the three rivers). The results of bathing in this
holy spot are instantaneous and miraculous, indeed
none can gain enlightenment without the company of
saints.[59] For the Viraśaivas the spiritual community is also important. Basava exclaims, 'How
can I, Lord, describe the joy that comes out of
communion with your saints?';[60] and the 'great
House' at Kalyāna which became a meeting place for
all who sought his teaching assumes a special
significance in the early literature of the movement. In Śūnyasampādane this great house is described in mystical terms and it is said to have
installed the 'empire of devotion' on this earth.[61]
Similarly the assembly hall in the 'great House',
known as the 'Hall of Experience' (*Anubhava
Maṇṭapa*) becomes a synonym for the gatherings or
Satsangas which took place around Basavanna in
Kalyāna. Yet another extension of the idea of the
spiritual community among the Vīraśaivas is to be
found in the institution of Maṭhas or monasteries,
which in some respects resemble the Buddhist Sanghas,
while retaining specifically Śaiva character.

22

Around the Guru and his congregation, the Satsanga, the new styles of worship called forth new symbols. In the visual field one thinks at once of the images of the Gods, and the ways in which their worship was understood. When an image is properly made and installed in accordance with the Śāstras, its nature is such that it becomes charged with power, becomes a presence, a theophany for the worshipper. Just as meditation upon a deity as seated within the spiritual centres of the body emphasises the immanent aspect, so does meditation upon an external image serve to focus the worshipper's mind upon the Transcendent. The image becomes a symbol of power. It is spoken of in various ways, sometimes in terms of a light which leads to the beyond (para), or as a mirror from whose centre the ineffable Nirguṇa aspect of God shines forth.[62] The postures, hand-mudras, attributes held in the hands of the icons, all become endowed with symbolic meaning. The Śilpa Śāstras give a precise idea of the way in which the deity is to be inducted into a finished icon. For example the Viṣṇudharmottara Purāṇa, one of the oldest such treatises, attempts to answer the question how the all-pervasive Viṣṇu, who is both para (beyond) and apara (not beyond), can come to reside in an image. Its answer is that

'the only reason for inducting him is for the mental satisfaction of the devotees. He does not need or want his image, but he concedes it to satisfy their devotion (bhakti), and as a gracious favour (anugraha). He who has no body comes to assume one so that his devotee can meditate upon this, because it is difficult to meditate upon what is formless'.[63]

Such explanations are not uncommonly met with and follow naturally upon the Bhagavadgītā's recommendation that devotion to the manifested form is to be preferred to that of the imperishable un-

manifest (*akṣara avyakta*), because difficult to
reach and tread is the way of the unmanifested.[64]
The images or forms of the Gods thus become a
major group of visual symbols.

We saw at the beginning that the conceptual
framework of religious symbols in India can be
connected with the relations of names and forms to
the Creator. The names of deities, from the time
of the Rigveda onwards, formed a fruitful pool for
the creation of religious symbols. In the post-
Upaniṣadic period the same process continues, and
with it a new cult of the divine Name. This symbol
is interesting and relevant for our purpose. The
cult doubtless developed out of earlier beginnings.
At the start, already in the Brāhmaṇa period it is
in evidence in the Śatarudrīya, the hundred names
of Rudra,[65] and it develops in the whole genre of
stuti or *stotra* literature.[66] Particularly in the
great devotional sects, the Śaiva and Vaiṣṇava,
the cult of the Name gained in importance, and in
the Mahābhārata we find lists of the thousand
names of both Viṣṇu and Śiva. In the Purāṇas the
divine Name is spoken of with great reverence as a
means to the destruction of sins; and the achievement of devotion, is said to be by repetition and
remembrance of the Name. The cult reaches its
climax in the medieval period when such saints as
Nānak and Kabīr elevate the name to an abstract
status. It is no longer a particular name, even
that of the chosen deity, which is important, but
the Name itself, as a symbol of God. Hence it is
spoken of as Satinām, the Name which is truth or
being itself.[67] But there is no fundamental difference between this 'Nirguṇa' usage and that of
the 'Saguṇa' saints. The common feature is that
now the Name is no ordinary name, but the Name of
God, and its repetition yields wonderful results
to the devotee. Both the actual names of God, such
as Hari, Rām, Śiva, etc., and the Name itself fill
the role of religious symbols, pointing beyond

24

themselves and beyond this world, and participating in the power to which they point. As we saw above Tulsīdās sang of the importance of the divine Name as greater than either the Nirguṇa or Saguṇa aspects of God, because it could make God accessible to man. His works, and the writings of other saints of the past two millennia, abound with his expressions of the wonder and power of the Name. This Name is therefore a symbol of very great power, pointing towards God, and yielding, like a Kalpataru or wish-granting tree, marvellous joy to the worshipper.

The last symbol I shall discuss is one of the most perplexing and problematic. Just as Śaivism in some ways epitomises Indian religion, so does the Śivalinga combine within itself many aspects of the Indian religious symbol. The origin of the cult of the Linga is lost in obscurity. Certain stone objects discovered in the excavations of Mohenjo-daro and Harappa have forms very similar to those of Lingas of the past two millennia. Their religious character is suggested by their find spots, which in almost all cases appear to have been in buildings with some special function. Of particular interest is a small group of beautifully made stones and hemispherical bases, bearing in one case the trefoil pattern, which recall Lingas and their *pīṭhas* or mountings. In the present state of knowledge it is not possible to affirm that these Harappan objects are stylised phalli, or that they have any connection with the Linga, but there appears to be a strong probability of some such association.

The word Linga is derived from the root √*lag*. adhere or attach, and its basic meaning is generally held to be 'mark, sign, badge, emblem'. From this base a number of extensions occur having more or less clear connections. Thus in logic *Linga* signifies the 'invariable mark which proves the existence of anything in an object'; in

25

Vedānta it is used in the phrase *Linga śarīra* for
the subtle body which accompanies a *jīva* in its
transmigration from birth to birth; in Sānkhya as
a synonym for Prakriti 'the eternal procreative
germ'. In grammar it is used as a technical term,
with the meaning of gender; and it is also used as
a technical term in rhetoric and other branches of
knowledge and science. Its meaning 'male organ of
generation' is likewise held to be an extension
which only comes into use at a comparatively later
date. The original meaning is found in the
Upaniṣads, for example in Śvetāśvatara Upaniṣad[68]
when it is said of Rudra-Śiva that he has no Linga,
no attribute. In the same vein the Upaniṣad speaks
of his having no name and no form. The Kaṭhopaniṣad also describes Brahman as 'Puruṣa and *Alinga*'.[69]
Thus it appears that the root meaning of Linga already anticipates its later use as a synonym for
symbol. How then did the word come to mean phallus?
and how did this meaning become associated with
Śiva?

There are widely divergent views on these
questions. It is not infrequently maintained that
Linga has never been used as a theological term in
any but its root meaning, and that the extension
to mean phallus has never been employed with reference to Śiva. But this appears to be special
pleading. Among the earliest passages relating to
the matter we may quote the Mahābhārata.[70] Here
Upamanyu remarks that offspring are not marked
with the lotus, wheel or *vajra*, that is to say
with the emblems of Brahmā, Viṣṇu or Indra, but
with the *linga* (male sex mark) and *bhaga* (female
sex mark, vulva). That all women are marked with
the latter because they are born of the Goddess,
and all men with the former because they are born
of Śiva. These are their manifest signs; all males
are from Śiva, all females from Umā. From their
two bodies issued all things, moving and unmoving.
Therefore the Linga is the *mark* of Śiva. This

26

passage is probably one of the later parts of the
text, and may be assigned to the early centuries
A.D., to the Kuṣāna-Gupta epoch. The earliest
datable representations of the Śiva linga belong
to this age, and it is noteworthy that most of the
early examples are naturalistic representations of
the phallus. The well-known Linga from Gudimallam
in South India serves to show this. Even in later
examples, from Gupta times, it is customary for
certain lines to be engraved on the stylised
Linga, illustrating their derivation from the
earlier naturalistic form. In passages written
from an expressly Śaivite point of view Śiva is
often spoken of as the Creator of the Universe, no
less than its ultimate destroyer, and this too,
finds expression in Śaivite cosmology. According
to later Śaivite thought the universe evolves as a
cosmic process, which begins with the ultimate
category (tattva), Parasamvit, or Paramaśiva, the
ultimate reality; and unfolds itself in its first
movements to Śivatattva (the first) and to
Śaktitattva the second.[71] Already at this level
there is a differentiation analogous to sexual
differentiation between Śiva (m.) and Śakti (f.),
and the latter is regarded as the creative power
or energy of God. In the further evolutionary
process these two recur at lower levels, emerging
as Puruṣa (m.) and Prakriti (f.) of the Sānkhya
system. The remaining tattvas correspond with
those of the Sānkhya system. These are found in
their evolved form in the Śānti Parva of the
Mahābhārata and in the Sānkhya Kārikas of Īśvara
Kriṣṇa, both presumably belonging to the early
centuries A.D. Thus the union of the instrumental
cause (Śiva) and the material cause (Śakti) may be
seen as analogous to the differentiation of sex in
creation. This development gave rise to a whole
ancient Indian philosophy of sex which finds expression in what later became known as Tantrism.
Not only the sex marks, but even the sex act be-

came incorporated into the realm of Indian religious symbolism, pointing analogically towards an aspect of cosmic evolution and to profound theological insights. That the erect phallus was associated with Śiva and his procreative activities, at least by some sects, is clear from another episode in the Mahābhārata.[72] Here Kriṣṇa relates how Brahmā ordered Śiva to create all beings, and when Śiva delayed, entering the waters and performing austerities, he created another great creator who forthwith performed the task. When Śiva emerged from his sleep beneath the waters and saw what had happened, he was angered and cut off his penis, throwing it down onto the ground where it remained standing erect. When Brahmā asked why he had done such a thing Śiva replied, 'You gave the task of creating offspring to another, what shall I do with this now?' This story further provides a clear attempt to explain or justify the Śivalingas which in the early centuries A.D. began to be installed in temples. From Kuṣāna times Śiva is frequently shown in iconic form as ithyphallic, even in his half female Ardhanārīśvara form. Śiva's ithyphallism (ūrdhvaretas) has always been open to different interpretations, in terms of sexual activity and procreation on the one hand and austerity, continence and the sublimation of sexual energy for spiritual ends on the other.[73]

The upshot of this tangled and confusing discussion is that, whether or not there is any connection between the stone objects of the Indus civilization and the later Linga, and whether the earlier use was restricted to the basic meaning 'mark or sign', the beginning of the iconographic use of the Linga coincides with the Kuṣāna period when Śiva is frequently shown as ithyphallic and when this feature is associated in the Mahābhārata with the cult of the Linga and with Śiva's role as creator of offspring. It is scarcely necessary for

28

me to remark upon the considerable interest of
these episodes in terms of their theological
significance, but I wish now to proceed to a brief
notice of the development which took place in
later centuries in the use of Linga in its root
meaning of mark, and of its explicit extension to
refer to a symbol pointing towards God.

It is certainly remarkable that already in
ancient times the chief use of Linga appears to
have been in its symbolic sense, at least in some
sects. Recalling the Upaniṣadic use, the Linga
Purāṇa states that the *alinga* (that which is without attributes) is the basis of the *linga*, the unmanifested (*avyakta*) is called the *linga*; Śiva is
alinga (without attributes), and the *linga* is said
to be Śaiva (belonging to Śiva, or of the Śaiva
sect).[74] The Purāṇa also states that the image of
the world created itself from the *alinga* as the
linga.[75] In whole bodies of literature the phallic
meaning is absent, and it is not difficult to make
a case for the wider relevence of the symbolic
meaning. It is difficult for us in an age whose
thought has been heavily influenced by Freud and
Reich to believe that the phallic meaning is not
the basic one, but this is what existing evidence
leads us to conclude.

To illustrate only one example of the later
usage I shall quote some passages from the Vīraśaivas who flourished in Karnāṭaka from the 12th
century. In their writing we find frequent references to four things, *guru*, *linga*, *jangama* and
prasāda. Each one is used as a religious symbol.
The second and third are related to each other,
the Linga being sometimes described as either
sthāvara (fixed) when it is installed in a temple,
or *jangama* (moving). The moving Linga however is
an enlightened saint and as a symbol may be compared to the guru.[76] The word Linga is frequently
translated or substituted in the Kannada texts by
a local word *kuṟuhu* which too means symbol.[77] The

29

symbol operates at three levels, the gross, subtle
and causal, and three terms are used, *iṣṭalinga,
prāṇalinga* and *bhāvalinga*. The *iṣṭalinga* takes the
form of a small amulet enclosing a tiny Linga. It
is presented to the disciple by the guru during
initiation and is henceforward worn at all times,
except when held on the palm during worship and
meditation. It is the only visual image employed
by the Vīraśaivas as even the fixed Lingas in the
temples are looked down on and other images are
not used at all. From its base at the gross level,
the *iṣṭalinga* is a symbol for the formless and
stainless God. During initiation the guru symbolises the two higher levels by imparting the six-
lettered mantra (*Oṃ namaḥ Śivāya*) and by placing
his hand upon the initiate's head. The symbolism
is beautifully described by the early saints.
Toṇṭada Siddhalinga writes:

> The holy Guru, giving form to the void, in-
> stalled it in my palm,
> Fashioning the void into formless form, merged
> it into my breath (*prāṇa*)
> Invoking the void of void and calling it void,
> immersed it in my will (*bhāva*)
> Wearing it in my palm, mind and will I realised
> the
> Consubstantial union of *anga* (body) and *linga*.[78]

The symbol participates in the power to which it
points and Vīraśaiva literature abounds with testi-
mony: the Linga is full of radiance and it gener-
ates a great light. Another writer says:

> In the heart of my palm the Guru showed
> The symbol of the immaculate supreme;
> In the heart of the symbol
> He showed the spark of consciousness;
> In the heart of the spark
> He showed the light of supreme knowledge;
> In the sublimity of that light
> He showed me himself in me.[79]

Its symbolic nature is clear in Basavanna's
Vacanas: for example, the several seats of the
great Linga are only its names; but the Linga itself is neither form nor formlessness.[80] Linga
cannot be grasped by the Vedas or the Śāstras, and
is beyond all logic. All is contained in Linga,
the ground and origin, it has no beginning, middle
or end.[81]

I hope that these few quotations will serve to
show the sublime nature of this symbol for the
Vīraśaivas.

I come now to the final section of this paper,
in which I shall consider in very summary fashion
the typology of the Indian religious symbols, in
the light of the types proposed by Tillich. First
there is the broad division into Transcendent and
Immanent levels, the former coinciding with
symbols which, as far as anything can do, point
directly towards God; the latter pointing towards
the manifestations of God in space and time. In
the Indian context it might be helpful to sub-
stitute for these categories the names Nirguṇa
symbols and Saguṇa symbols. Within the Nirguṇa
symbols the first group are those which refer
directly to God. In Indian theology they would
seem to divide into several classes: first comes
the word *Brahman*, which more than any other
equates to the theological usage 'God', and which
as we have seen is universally regarded as a
Nirguṇa level, beyond all predication and describ-
able only through negatives. The origin of the
term (as we noticed in passing) is mysterious, and
deserves more comment than we have been able to
give it. The second major Nirguṇa symbol is *Oṃ*,
that 'most grand' name of God. A third symbol must
be *Linga*, which alone among visual symbols ap-
proaches the Nirguna level, and which combines
with the visual and immanent elements of its meaning a transcendent level. Another term which
deserves inclusion in this group is *Śūnya*, Void.

31

I must confess myself in some doubt as to whether
it is right to include within this first group
another subdivision starting with Ātman, Self, and
including its extensions Paramātman, Adhyātman,
and in the same line the terms Antaryāmī, Tajjalān,
and Kṣetrajña. Also deserving consideration are
the usages stressing the Nirguṇa aspect of names
of God such as Śiva, Viṣṇu, Rām, etc.

The second group of the Nirguṇa symbols is that
referring to the divine attributes. Here three
stand out above all others, Sat, Cit, and Ānanda.
Brahman is referred to already in the Upaniṣads as
Sat, being or Being itself; Cit, consciousness
itself; and Ānanda, bliss itself. In the course of
time there are other attributes, but the distinc-
tion of these from the activities of God is often
not clearly analysed, and I am not prepared to
discuss them. The description of God's activities
is partly carried on at the mythological level, at
any rate in later literature. The role of God as
Creator, Preserver and Destroyer of the Universe
is generally of such an order. Other activities
are more clearly theological. Among these the
exercise of Love, Compassion, and Grace stand out.

The second category is of Saguṇa symbols. In
presenting these I must preface my remarks by
calling attention to the different signification
of the words space and time in the Indian context.[82] By space is included not only this world,
but all the other levels of world, above and
below; and by time is meant not only time which
we can record as human beings, but cosmic time,
cyclic time, etc. Thus the manifestations of the
holy in space and time involve a broader sense of
history and time than we should normally allow and
consequently much which we should not allow as
historical finds place. Here history and mythology
merge with each other. First must come the manifestations of God as Viṣṇu, Śiva, etc., of whatever kind. Terms such as Īśa, Lord; Bhagavān,

Blessed one, are ambivalent, sharing both Nirguṇa
and Saguṇa levels. The second group consists of
incarnations. Under this heading we include the
incarnations of Viṣṇu as they are recorded in the
Purāṇas, etc., also the mythological appearances
of Śiva, Viṣṇu, etc., as they are described in the
Purāṇas. These are no less symbols, and we have
already noticed their ambivalence as symbols at
the Nirguṇa level. Under this category, but in a
separate sub-group to the incarnations and mythological manifestations, comes a third set including, since Vedic times, Fire, Agni, and Sun, Sūrya,
etc. Also in a separate group within the first
division of the Saguṇa symbols come such entities
as Name, Speech, Breath, Sound, etc., whose
symbolic role we have noticed.

The second broad division according to Tillich
consists of 'sacramental' symbols. I am not very
happy with this term, but for want of a better, I
have retained it. Under this heading I include
Yajña, Sacrifice, the Guru (who might also be included as an incarnatory symbol), Initiation,
Dīkṣa; Brahmacarya; the spiritual community,
Satsanga; and Grace, Prasāda. The final group of
Saguṇa symbols are the sign-symbols, and here
there is a great number, since almost everything
can for a time be accorded symbolical status.
Among important examples we may note the Conch and
Wheel (Śankha and Cakra), which are not only
attributes of Viṣṇu, but have also a definite
symbolic status; the lotus; the Triśūla (of Śiva);
etc. In the Purāṇas and among their expositors
almost every sentence contains elements of secondary symbolic significance, which may be included
in this category; just as almost every trait of a
deity, in iconic form, and every episode represented in sculpture or paint, is similarly open
to a secondary symbolic interpretation. These
elements mainly belong to the class of sign-
symbols.

In conclusion let me say, that Tillich's description of religious symbols appears to be valuable in the analysis of Indian theology, even if the analysis which it involves is largely not present in Indian thought itself; and Tillich's typology of symbols too appears to be, with some modifications, very suitable for the discussion of Indian religious symbols.

2. THE WORLD TO COME. A TWO-THOUSAND YEAR OLD PAINTING FROM CHINA

Michael Loewe

OF THE MANY archaeological discoveries reported from China in the last few years, the two-thousand year old painting from tomb no.1 Ma-wang-tui, Hu-nan province, can claim with some justice to be one of the most valuable. It was this tomb which contained the body of a woman in a perfect state of preservation, and the silk painting was found draped, face downwards, over the innermost of the four coffins in which she had been so reverently interred. Subsequent finds have made it almost certain that the woman can be identified as the first countess of Tai. Her husband had held a provincial appointment at the outset of the Western Han dynasty (202 B.C. to A.D. 8) and died in 186 B.C. His widow survived him for at least a dozen years, and the painting, which is now matched by a similar one that was found in an adjoining tomb, may be dated at c.168 B.C. The painting is well preserved, and the colours, either of vegetable or mineral dyes, are still highly vivid. The overall length of the painting is 2.05 metres; it is 92 cm wide at the top, and slightly half that width at the foot.

Probably the painting had been made for carriage in the countess' funeral procession, before being consigned to its final resting place. Its theme and purpose may be inferred from a number of passages in Chinese literature which reveal contemporary ideas of life and death. Many of the details of the painting refer to the very rich mythology of southern China that is best known from a collection of poems that date from the Han period or somewhat earlier,[1] and the painting forms a valuable aid to the elucidation of the more abstruse passages of those texts.

The interpretation of the painting which follows depends partly upon literary evidence; partly on our understanding of Chinese religious beliefs of the second century B.C.; and partly on comparison with subsequent traditional funerary practice. It should perhaps be stressed that the interpretation does not agree in all respects with the views that have been put forward by several Chinese scholars.[2]

Shaped like a T, the painting consists of two parts, one horizontal and one vertical, and the artist probably intended a viewer's eye to move slowly from the foot to the head. The purpose of the painting is to escort the soul (*hun*) of the countess to paradise, and the artist guides the soul to its destination through a number of discrete stages that are separated into distinct tableaux. The journey proceeds from earth to paradise by way of P'eng-lai, one of the islands of the immortals believed to lie in the seas east of China. P'eng-lai was sometimes described as the Isle of the Pot; its inhabitants were deemed to be immortal and to possess those elixirs of which a dose could confer the blessing of immortality. Once a person had tasted these elixirs he could proceed to paradise for the enjoyment of a life everlasting.

The vertical part of the painting shows the Island of P'eng-lai or the Pot. The sides of the pot are formed by two dragons; there is a horizontal, flat base at the foot, and a lid which carries flanges of the type that are seen on contemporary pots of lacquer-ware, ceramic or bronze. The shape of such pots is very similar to that seen in the painting. The sinuous curves of the two dragons' bodies are entwined together in a ring, which is reminiscent of the rings that are often attached to Han pots for use in carriage. It also serves to separate the vertical part of the painting into two tableaux, in the same way as

图三八　彩绘帛画（约 ¹/₇）

Painting on silk, found in no.1 tomb, Ma-weng-tui
(Hu-nam province). *From the official report on the
site (Peking, 1973).*

the surfaces of contemporary pots are decorated
with two separated bands of embellishment.

A pair of turtles press firmly against the
sides of the pot. According to Chinese mythology,
there was once a fear that the Island of P'eng-lai
would drift away from its position, to be lost
forever beyond the confines of the universe. So
the Supreme Power gave orders for the island to
be made fast, and a set of turtles, working in
teams by rota, made sure that the base was se-
curely anchored. The two leviathans that are seen
at the base of the painting indicate that the Pot
is situated in the sea.

The progress of the countess possibly starts
with the carriage of her coffin into the scene of
the lower tableau. It may be seen resting on short
stilts on the ground, in the far distance; and the
poles whereby it was carried into its position are
still in place. From here we move forward to the
main scene of the lower tableau. The countess,
attended by five servants, partakes of a solemn
feast, served by a white-robed attendant who is
seen at the left of the tableau. One of the dis-
tinctive features of the Island of P'eng-lai was
that all the inhabitants, human and animal alike,
were coloured white; and it is possible that the
two sets of vessels that stand before the banquet
are those in which the elixirs had been prepared
or preserved.

The countess, then, had been attended by five
servants, and we may note that these vessels are
divided into one set of two, on the left, and one
set of three, on the right. Above the canopy and
ring which surmount this scene, there is a stair-
way, set obliquely so as to infuse movement into
the painting, and to lead our pilgrims to the
upper tableau of the lower part of the painting.
This is the final stage before the ascent to paradise. The countess stands clothed in brilliantly
coloured silks; three pearls adorn her headdress,

38

as befits her rank, and there can be little doubt
that we are gazing at a portrait of the lady. Her
two sets of attendants, two and three, anxiously
provide her with her last needs; for the final
stage of the journey which yet awaits her may be
beset by dangers. The gate-posts of paradise are
guarded by stern wardens who refuse admittance
save to the elect; and ferocious beasts stand by
to assist them in their watch.

But the soul of the countess is ready for these
hazards, and the artist conducts her through the
portals to the wide scene of paradise that occupies the upper part of the painting. This is a
realm inhabited by the Sun and the Moon, duly
shown with their respective attributes, i.e. the
two legged (later three legged) bird for the sun,
and the toad and hare for the moon. In other early
Chinese works of art, where the moon is shown in
full face, these emblems are necessary for purposes of identification. In the painting under
study the sun is shown at the head of the Fu-sang,
or tree of paradise, up whose branches seven
smaller suns are climbing. The toad that dances so
happily within the moon is associated with the
figure of a woman, who rests on the wing of a
dragon, gazing up towards the crescent. The figure
has been identified as that of Heng O, who was
said to have stolen the drug of immortality as a
present for her husband; but on second thoughts
she decided to consume the elixir herself, and was
duly carried to eternity in the moon, being transformed into a toad for the purpose.

At the central apex of the painting, the climax
which the viewer's eye will eventually reach,
there stands a female figure, blue-robed, and
attended by two sets of cranes, two to the left
and three to the right. The figure is not altogether human, for the trunk is joined, not to a
pair of legs, but to a serpentine coil whose
twists and curls form a strikingly beautiful

pattern. Several attempts have been made to identify this figure with creatures who are described
in Chinese mythology, and some commentators regard
the figure as male. But it seems all too clear
that here we see the countess for the last time,
safely brought to her destination. She has
sloughed off the mortal coils in which we last saw
her; and perhaps her serpentine form alludes to
the ease with which this metamorphosis can be
achieved by creatures such as snakes. Beneath her
there is a bell suspended by legendary figures who
may not be identified; and the bell supports a
dish from which there arise aromas or vapours that
attract the attention of two other birds. Possibly
the dish was hung there to catch the honeydew of
paradise, whose blessings were well-known in the
world below and frequently sought by those who
aspired to a life of immortality.

The foregoing interpretation of the painting
found in tomb no.1, Ma-wang-tui, cannot explain
all the detail of this singularly rich work of art;
and it is likely that many features will long
remain matters of controversy in the learned world.
The painting was completed perhaps two and a half
centuries before Buddhism reached China; it is
also dated about a century before the statesmen of
the Han dynasty succeeded in fostering certain
religious views and philosophical ideas so as to
form the orthodox framework of imperial China.
Such Confucian orthodoxy promoted the classical
and regular outlook of the north rather than the
romantic approach of the south that is represented
in the painting; but while the southern type of
culture was somewhat eclipsed in official eyes,
its strength never waned on a popular level, as may
be testified by the history of Taoist practices in
China. The painting is a remarkable piece of evidence of the strength of early Chinese beliefs in
the life hereafter.

3. THE OLD ENGLISH RUNIC PATERNOSTER

Eric J.Sharpe

Min son, jag satt här i så månget år
och är med Guds hjälp välbehållen.
Den rätt kan läsa sitt Fader vår,
han rädes varken fan eller trollen,
Fast det är mörkt långt, långt bort i skogen.

Erik Gustaf Geijer, *Den lilla kolargossen*

ERIK GUSTAF GEIJER'S poem about the charcoal-
burner's son, shuddering his way through the
forest carrying his father's supper, is perhaps
not one of the masterpieces of world literature.
But it rings true to anyone who has ever experienced the Scandinavian forests, by day or by night:
especially by night. The experience of absolute
darkness, unlit by any artificial means, is one of
the many human experiences that urbanization has
made increasingly rare for most of us; but you may
still find it in those forests, sometimes less
than a stone's throw from a busy main road or rail-
way. Move a little farther in, and darkness is
joined by silence — at which point imagination
(or perception, according to the theory you favour)
takes over.

The charcoal-burner's son had a fearful walk
through the forest. His terrors were aroused not
only by the thought of the bears and the wolves,
but even more by the thought of the unseen — the
powers, the elves and trolls, the ghosts and the
goblins with which the forest teemed. But then he
found his father, and was at once reassured:

My son, I have sat here for many a year,
And am by God's grace, safe and calm;
I say 'Our Father' to banish my fear,
Neither devil nor trolls do me harm,
Though it is dark deep, deep in the forest.

In the most dangerous of places, nothing but the most powerful of protections would suffice. That protection was the Lord's Prayer, the *Pater Noster*, 'Our Father which art in heaven...'

The dangers of the forest, now somewhat neutralised by distance and electricity, are still theoretically recognised in Scandinavia. In Sweden, when a child is baptised, one of the prayers offered after the actual baptism says:

Thou hast by thy fatherly grace received this infant as thy child: keep him (her) in thy love. He must travel through a dangerous world: lead him along thy paths. His time is in thy hands: be near him always...

These words 'He must travel through a dangerous world' were once to be taken literally. The belief which they still represent is essentially that of the dweller in the forest clearing, with the tangible darkness and all its hidden powers forever pressing in on a very vulnerable mortal. The enemy was always on the watch, like a roaring lion seeking whom he might devour — always prepared and eager to open another bridgehead in the eternal war of light and darkness. This belief is still reflected in many ways, but nowhere more clearly than in Swedish Hymn 266, 'Tva väldiga strider om människans själ' — 'Two mighty ones battle for the soul of man'. Does this, then, mean that the traditional or the so-called popular Christianity of the North was (and perhaps still is) dualist? Indeed it does, though that is not a question I propose to discuss further on this occasion.

Let us accept that a battle was being fought, with the prize the soul of man. In theory, this battle was no more fierce in one place than in another; and yet there were sensitive points. The forest, for instance, where the poor shivering mortal might simply be swallowed up by a darkness that just could not be doubted, if he did not take

42

counter measures. Geijer knew very well what, of
the available counter measures, was the most
effective in this setting: 'Fader vår, som är i
himmelen, helgat varde ditt namn...' — 'Our Father,
which art in heaven, hallowed be thy name'. The
forest dweller or worker might of course have had
other prophylactics, but these need not concern us.
It is at the Lord's Prayer that we must pause. Not
exclusively the Lord's Prayer as known and used in
Scandinavia (though some of my material will come
from Scandinavia), but an Old English interpretation of the Lord's Prayer in Latin, the *Pater
Noster*.

First, though, it might be as well to admit
that this will be a folklore study only by impli-
cation, and that I have not really tried to follow
up the folklore tradition as it relates to the
Lord's Prayer. Others of you no doubt know this
material well enough already. I do have a Lord's
Prayer tinily, and quite legibly, inscribed upon a
Victorian threepenny piece to show that the
prophylactic quality of the Lord's Prayer is not
dead. I should also like to guard myself against
the accusation of being unconcerned with the
Christian theological implications of this subject
by offering a propitiatory (or perhaps a prophylactic) quotation from a fairly recent work of
German theology:

> For a single word, when it takes place, can lay
> complete hold of us and carry us through every-
> thing — into the darkness, certainly, yet with
> the irrefutable expectation: darkness is not
> dark to thee. And the name when it is called...
> has the *power* to come home to me completely as a
> person, and gives me the *freedom* to respond
> completely as a person.[1]

Intellectualised — certainly; indistinct — certainly; but the key concepts of darkness, power
and freedom are still there. Apparently a word can

still rescue the believer from darkness, and through its power convey the one who uses it in trust, into a realm of freedom. The Germanic priorities have, it seems, been maintained in spite of everything.

It is now high time to turn from these generalities to the main theme of my paper, the Old English Runic Paternoster — a fearsome combination of words! Several years ago, I came across, in a local second-hand book shop, a copy of J.M.Kemble's 1848 edition of *The Dialogue of Salomon and Saturnus*, a ninth or tenth century Old English document (or rather group of documents) of which I must confess that I had not at that time previously heard. I bought it on an impulse, and have been intrigued by it ever since. It may be that others are in the same position of ignorance about 'Salomon and Saturn' as I was when I bought it; and so I shall begin by giving a short summary of the contents of the first of the dialogues, that known as Poem I.[2]

The partners in the dialogue are, of course, the ancient king of Israel, Solomon, the man of proverbial wisdom; and Saturn, whose origins and character are not altogether transparent.[3] For our present purposes, however, it is perhaps enough to say that he appears to represent Time (Father Time, even), and that he is in possession of the fulness of pagan wisdom, more or less as Solomon possesses Judaeo-Christian wisdom. Saturn has come seeking Solomon because he has recognised that his own (Saturn's) wisdom is deficient at one vital point. He has been, he says, to Lybia and Crete, and even to India; but he has not succeeded in learning the most powerful of all the powerful writings. Will Solomon help him?

Solomon, in his reply, does not at once identify the writing in question (which you will no doubt have guessed by now is the *Pater Noster*), but says that whoever does not know 'the canticle' is in a

44

sorry plight, since in the day of doom the 'fearful dragon' will simply swallow him up, unprotected as he is, as he topples from Michael's balances. Saturn asks, 'Who may then open the doors of the kingdom of heaven?' Solomon replies, 'The palm-twigged Pater Noster.'[4]

> Therefore hath the canticle
> over all Christ's books
> the greatest repute:
> it teacheth the scriptures,
> with voice it directeth,
> and its place it holdeth,
> heaven-kingdom's
> arms it wieldeth.

But, asks Saturn, how does it achieve these wonderful ends? 'No man knoweth,' he says (and one can understand him), 'how my spirit sinks labouring over books.' Why should this scripture be so different from all the others?

There follows Solomon's *tour de force*, as he answers this question in a long exposition, extolling all the manifold virtues of the *Pater Noster*. Curiously, he does not say what the prayer actually contains, nor does he quote any part of it except its first two words, and then only in Latin. One ought not, I am sure, conclude that the writer did not actually know the *Pater Noster*, but it is certainly possible that he did not want its text to be communicated to the uninitiated. At all events, there is no mention of the hallowing of the Divine Name, the coming of the Kingdom, the forgiving of one's enemies. Instead there is a remarkable panegyric:

> It is the leech of the lame,
> the light of the blind,
> it is also the door of the deaf,
> the tongue of the dumb,
> the shield of the guilty,
> the dwelling of the Creator...

— leading on to an even more remarkable section, which contains the real justification for this present paper.

In a passage of some 120 half-lines, the letters forming the words PATER NOSTER and individual letters from the later parts of the prayer are expounded, in the order in which they occur, *a letter at a time*.[5] That in itself is remarkable enough, but still more remarkable is the fact that each letter is reproduced both as a Roman letter and as an Anglo-Saxon rune. Solomon informs Saturn that each symbol separately exercises a particular type of influence over the powers of evil, afflicting the devil with a pain or other discomfort. To say PATER NOSTER, then, is to bring a whole arsenal of powerful weapons to bear on the enemy of God and man, the 'fighting fiend', the devil. I cannot quote the entire passage, but I can provide a taste of it:

> ...he that will earnestly
> this God's-word
> sing in sooth,
> and him will ever
> love without crime,
> he may the hated spirit,
> the fighting fiend
> bring to flight,
> if thou at first over him
> earnestly bringest
> Prologa prima
> whose name is P: [ðam is ᛈ P nama:]
> the warrior has
> a long rod,
> with a golden goad,
> and ever the grim fiend
> fierce-minded smiteth;
> and on his track pursueth
> A with mighty power, [ᚾ A ofermægene]
> and him also beateth.

T plagueth him, and him [↑ T hine teswað...]
in the tongue stabbeth,
twisteth his throat for him
and his cheeks breaketh.
E afflicteth him, [ᛗ E hine yflað]
as he ever will
fastly stand against
every foe;
then little to his pleasure, R [ðonne hine on
                                        unðanc, ᚱ R]
shall angrily seek him;
the prince of letters
shall soon whirl
the fiend by his hair,
he will let the flint break
the phantasm's shanks;
never shall he witness
the comfort of his limbs,
nor shall any leech be good for him.
Then shall he depart under the welkin,
his fortress seek
covered with darkness,
at any rate he will be sad at heart,
when he hanging
hell shall wish for,
the narrowest
of realms;
......
then cometh S, [ðonne ᚻ S cymeð]
the prince of angels,
the staff of glory,
he shall clutch the angry
fiend by the feet,
shall dash his forward cheek
on the strong stone,
and scatter his teeth
around the crowds of hell:
each one shall hide himself
in the indistinctness of shadow;

the fiend shall he trouble,
Satan's thane
made very still.[6]

Now all this may strike the commentator as very
curious indeed, and some worthy linguists and
historians of literature have been hard pressed to
know what to make of *Salomon and Saturn* as a
result. Kemble did not know whether or not he
ought to be laughing at it, and Menner one feels
to have looked down his nose at it, since it was
so obviously 'superstition'.[7] But I think we ought
to take it seriously. It was not meant as enter-
tainment, after all, but as a most serious piece
of practical theology. However, from our point of
view its main merit is that it brings together in
a quite remarkable way several different channels
of supernatural power, and serves as a symbol of
all of them simultaneously.

Curiously, the one dimension of the Lord's
Prayer which does not come out here is that of an
expression of personal devotion. No notice what-
soever seems to be taken of the prayer's biblical
origin, of the situation or situations in which it
was taught by Jesus, and of the separate elements
which go to make it up.[8] As I said earlier, it is
as though the unknown poet either does not know,
or wishes to keep very much to himself, the actual
contents of the prayer. Actually, though, I am not
convinced that it would be a very fruitful line of
enquiry to try to draw lines of connection between
the dialogue and the origins of the prayer. Its
ethos is Germanic through and through, and it is
to that cultural area we must look for our explanations.

The Pater Noster in this connection is first of
all an *incantation*.

I am sure that it is not necessary for me to do
much more than remind you of the power of incantations and of some of the rules governing their

use in the Germanic world. In the perpetual commerce between the world of men and the parallel world of the spirit-powers, there were certain more or less guaranteed modes of communication between the two. One of the most important of these was verbal, though it should be remembered that verbal modes in turn branch out into the two separate areas of oral and written communication. Taking the oral aspect first, a certain sound and order of words would come to be regarded as possessing power. Notice that the words would as a rule not be regarded as establishing a personal rapport with the spirits (though they might at times do so), but as exercising force upon them. Not *impersonal* force, but force emanating from a superior source, and proved in actual combat.

The manipulator of the incantation would not need to know anything about it save its sound, and later the letters out of which it was made up. The meaning (if it had meaning) would be no concern of his, or hers.

In the Germanic area the words were reinforced by a particular kind of declamation, which we should probably have to describe as 'screeching' — raising the voice to an abnormal pitch, and thereby passing into the domain of the spirits. Incantations of this type were called in Scandinavia *galdrar*, and for etymologists, the crowing of a cock is still in modern Swedish described by the verb *gala*, and again in Swedish, a common word for 'mad' is *galen*. The total impression is one of high-pressure, and possibly ecstatic (possibly again reinforced by alcohol or other drugs) utterance of a received formula. It might be added that even in such a state, the proprieties had to be observed, and there existed a special form of verse in Old Norse called *galdralag*.

The web of tradition in the Germanic world attributed the powers of incantation in particular to the god Odin, and you may read his *galdrar* in,

49

for instance, *Hávamál*. The connection between the god of the *galdrar* and the god of death is well known, and is emphasised in a slightly different context in *Grógaldr*, another Eddic poem in which the wraith of a departed wise woman is brought back for the specific purpose of teaching something of the art of incantation.

Now when in the beginning of this dialogue we find Saturn claiming to have combed the ancient world in search of books and their contents, I think we may safely suppose that he was really looking in the first instance for oral incantations — power-words — and in the second instance for written incantations — power-words the efficacy of which was doubled by being made permanent in writing. That the ancient and medieval worlds were full of both kinds of incantation is self-evident. For instance, Odin, the lord of the dead and the master of incantation was equally, and perhaps even more importantly, the master of the runes, the inventor of powerful writing (a point actually mentioned in *Salomon and Saturn*). He it is who reaches down from the gallows-tree to pluck up the runes from the ground.[9]

The survival of the incantation tradition in the North is fairly well documented, thanks to the work of folklorists. Sometimes these survivals give striking insights into what we might call the machinery behind the process, as for instance the case of the Swedish peasant woman who claimed in 1722 that she had learned certain incantations from a monk, Herr Jon, who had his 'prayers' written down in a little book. It is not only the fact that the tradition here had survived over at least two centuries, but that there is a clear link between written and oral power-words. Written down in a little book they may have been; but they needed to be pronounced before they could 'work'. Nevertheless the written incantation was powerful, though its power might be latent.

Of course the most startling thing about the Runic Pater Noster is precisely that it should have been expressed in runes. After all, were the runes not hopelessly pagan, and did the Church not possess the four-square Roman alphabet and the Latin language in which to express its doctrinal, devotional and legal treasures?[10]

We are trembling here on the brink of a very serious problem indeed in the history of religion in the north of Europe (and elsewhere in the world, for that matter). Here I can do little more than hint at it. Traditional interpretation of the so-called 'conversion' of northern Europe has been very seriously hampered by an over-fondness for thinking in terms of religious *systems*. Thus it tends to be supposed that there was a pagan Germanic system, which was replaced either suddenly or gradually by a Christian system, usually as a consequence of the conversion of a king or queen. It is the systems that bedevil the argument.[11] Eliminate systems, and you are half way to understanding the process by which new impulses from the Christian tradition combined in subtle and infinitely varied and variable ways with ancient impulses from the Germanic and Celtic heritages to form northern medieval Christianity as we (partly) know it. You may if you wish label the process 'syncretism', though systems are bound up with this notion, too. Certainly the type of faith and belief which emerged from the encounter was distinctively Germanic, and there is no better illustration of this than *Salomon and Saturn*.

There is nothing more Germanic than the symbolic use of the runes, and nothing more evocative of the Germanic past than the words 'rune' and 'runic'. As R.I.Page observes, 'The more emotive meanings of the words have attracted mystics, muddlers and cranks, who have enthusiastically discovered runes where none exist...'[12] The words are easily taken to mean 'magical' and

'mysterious', and there is indeed good reason why
this should be so, though the magic and the mystery could sometimes get out of hand, as in the
case of the writer in the 1840s who spoke of
'...a Runic or Buddhist cross...' on the Isle of
Man![13]

Concerning the actual origins of the runes we
know little enough. The consensus seems to be that
they originated as the result of a single creative
impulse, somewhere in North Italy. 'All we know,'
writes R.W.V.Elliott, 'is that in some Germanic
tribe some man had both the leisure...and the remarkable phonetic sense to create the futhark from
a North Italic model known to him somewhere in the
alpine regions in the period c. 250 to 150 B.C.'[14]
Elliott again is quite convinced that the runic
alphabet would never have been invented had it not
been needed for 'divination and lot-casting';
hence it was 'linked from the start with religious
beliefs and certain ritual practices'.[15] Other
scholars disagree, maintaining that the magical
use of runes was secondary and derivative. Personally I feel that any alphabet or other form of
writing was liable to be used in what we might
call a meta-literary way in the ancient world.
Most of them were, particularly by people who had
not actually mastered the arts of reading and writing.

At all events, throughout the Germanic world
runes were used, particularly between the 8th and
the 13th centuries A.D., for all manner of purposes connected with the exercise and control of
supernatural power. Not only for these purposes,
however. Some runic inscriptions are very straight-
forward — like the Gripsholm inscription from
Sweden, celebrating certain Vikings: '...They
voyaged manfully, to far lands seeking gold; and
in the East they fed the eagles; they died south-
ward in Särkland.'[16]

Even in these cases, of course, the runes might

well have exercised protection over the dead on behalf of the god of the dead. Protection, that is, against forces of evil and destruction. A similar protection would be needed in war; and hence weapons would be inscribed with runes — the name of the weapon and the name of the owner, for instance. Runic inscriptions might be used to mark roads and bridges, as well as graves and monuments — a practice which continued well on into Christian times in Sweden.

But in very many cases, there was belief in quite specific supernatural power attached to the runes. One does not need to look twice at an inscription like that of the Stentoften Stone, to discern the powers at work: 'This is the secret of the runes. Here I hid the runes of power, untroubled by angry sorcery. Whoever destroys this monument, will die by the magical arts.'[17] It is necessary to look twice, and more than twice, at the Lindholm amulet from Skåne, which bears the remarkable inscription: 'aaaaaaaarrrnnnbmutttalu'. This looks like a prentice rune-carver practicing his trade; and apart from the last word, *alu*, a magical word, nothing emerges of sense: but probably it is an expression of non-conceptual power, power merely through the *forming* of the runes.

It may seem (bearing in mind what I said a little while ago about patterns of conversion in the North) as though this would be one practice which the Christian Church would have been less than enthusiastic to see perpetuated. And indeed there is evidence from much later in time (for instance from seventeenth-century Iceland) which shows that runes were eventually looked upon as devilish, at least in some contexts. But even here, the basic impulse to gain protection by the use of written symbolism was merely transferred to that most Protestant of all holy books — not the Bible, but the hymnal. We know that in Sweden in comparatively recent times the hymnal could be used magic-

53

ally, pages being torn out and fastened over the
stall of a cow in calf or a cow with colic. Pages
might even be given to a cow to eat! As af Klintberg points out, 'The explanation is only in part
that these were sacred Christian words; already
the fact that they were made up of letters was
important.'[18] Superstition, perhaps: but after all,
what is superstition but religion without the
benefit of clergy?

Of course the runes were widely used by Christians before the Reformation. I do not intend to go
into the alliance between the symbolism of the
runes and that of the Cross, though a cross bearing a runic inscription was discovered some years
ago here in Lancaster, and many others are known
from the north of England and the south of Scotland.[19] Usually, though, this further dimension of
symbolism was not necessary. The runes themselves,
once found by Odin, had passed by conquest to the
hand of Christ the King, and were available to
those who were Christ's by baptism: 'I pray for
the aid of earth and high heaven,' says the Ribe
inscription from Denmark, 'Sun and Saint Mary and
God the King, that he lend me healing hand and
life tongue, for the healing of hurt when comfort
is called: from back and breast, from body and
limbs, from eyes and ears, from all that evil can
attack.'

But this is still not all. The runes collect-
ively were invested with power largely, it seems,
because they were written symbols; but beyond that,
every single rune was traditionally invested with
its own *peculiar* power, a belief no doubt traceable back to the pictograms from which the letters
had emerged. The precise nature of this specific
power is not always easy to describe. Our source
material is by no means as full as one might wish,
and the material we have — for instance, in the
various 'Runic Poems', Icelandic, Norwegian, Old
English and so on — does not always fit into neat

54

patterns.[20] Attempts have of course been made, and
made repeatedly, to reconcile one interpretation
with another along this line. Personally I am not
qualified to make any such attempt. It will be
enough for my present purposes if I try to bring
together a little of the material, restricting
myself mainly to some of the runes which in
Salomon and Saturn are used to spell the word
PATER.

The rune P comes first. Very little is said
about it in *Salomon and Saturn*: simply that 'the
warrior has a long rod, with a golden goad, and
ever the grim fiend fierce-minded smiteth'. It
sounds rather as though the rune is being compared
to a spear or javelin; and this may indeed be so,
on one level. But if we look at the Anglo-Saxon
Runic Poem, we find there the somewhat puzzling
information that this rune, Peorð, '...is a source
of recreation and amusement to the great, where
warriors sit blithely together in the banqueting-
hall'.[21] Schneider suggests that the reference is
probably to the game of dice, which is of course
known to have been a peculiar weakness of the Indo-
European mind. He in fact produces a most impress-
ive collection of evidence from various parts of
the Indo-European area to support his thesis,
after which he suggests that the pictographical
object of the rune might even have been a dice-
box.[22] He draws lines of comparison between the
idea of fate and the ideology of various games of
chance, from the Roman *alea fati* ('Dice of Fate')
and *alea belli* to such expressions as 'das
Schicksal hat die Hand im Spiele'. He might perhaps have added such English expressions as 'the
die is cast'.

Now clearly there is much more material which
might have been, and in Schneider's presentation
is, brought to bear on the subject of fate.[23] And
it might be mentioned that the veteran Swedish
runologist Sigurd Agrell interpreted this rune

quite differently, on a (probably wrong) derivation of *peoro* from the Latin *petra*, concluding
that since Mithra had been born from the rock, and
since the origin of the runic names is directly or
indirectly Mithraic, the meaning of this rune is a
symbol of the magical powers of the earth.[24]

Assuming that Schneider is right, however, that
the P-rune in the *Pater Noster* has to do with fate,
what is meant may be that the sovereign and in-
comprehensible will of God, which men call 'fate'
for want of a better word, is brought immediately
to bear on the Devil, to his discomfort. For fate
is not an impersonal adjunct to Deity, and still
less a power to which God himself must submit; it
is the direct expression of his power.

Very little is said in *Salomon and Saturn* about
the power of A, T and E, though each adds to the
trials and tribulations of the Devil. T in particular is a vicious weapon, stabbing the Devil's
tongue, breaking his jaw and strangling him all in
one.[25] T is as it happens the rune of the ancient
high god of war, *Tyr*, or *Tiw* (IE/tiwaz), and
certainly represents the eternal conflict of
cosmos and chaos. The shape of the rune could not
represent a spear more clearly than it does. The
message is that the Devil has come up against the
power of creation, against which his desire to
destroy and deny is bound to come to nothing.

The last rune of PATER, the R rune *rād* or *reið*,
is spoken of in ecstatic terms, as 'the prince of
letters', who will whirl the fiend by the hair,
break the devil's bones with 'the flint' and leave
the enemy desiring oblivion — an oblivion he will
never find. Reference to the various runic poems
shows that this particular rune is connected above
all with horses and with riding. The Anglo-Saxon
Runic Poem reads: 'Rad seems easy to every
warrior while he is indoors and very courageous to
him who traverses the high-roads on the back of a
stout horse.'[26] The Norwegian Runic Poem: 'Ræið

is said to be the worst thing for horses; reginn forged the finest sword.'[27] And the Icelandic: 'Riding = joy of the horseman/and speedy journey/ and toil of the steed.'[28]

It seems fairly obvious that we have been brought here into the sphere of activity of the ancient sun-god, and of his steeds and chariot. It might therefore be excusable if I were to launch into a consideration of sun-symbolism; but I do not intend to do so, save in one particular. Schneider again draws attention to the fact that there was in ancient Scandinavia a close relation- ship between the sun-cult and a particular kind of music, viz., the music of the *lur*, the bell of which might well take its place along with the *svastika* and the rings, circles and discs as a powerful sun-symbol.[29] Among the *hällristningar* of the Scandinavian past there are many *lur*-players;[30] while at the other end of the Indo-European spectrum the reader of the *Bhagavad Gītā* can scarcely fail to be struck by the care with which the blowing of various trumpets and horns is de- scribed at the beginning of the battle of Kuruk- shetra. Each of these — Pānchajanya of Krishna, Devadatta of Arjuna, Bhima's Paundra, Yudhisthira's Anantavijaya and so on — had its supernatural, as well as its acoustic, effect, on the enemies of order and right.[31] Thus the use of this rune has the effect of bringing an ancient cumulative (though possibly half-forgotten) tradition of power to bear on the enemy of mankind.

Again it should be mentioned, still in connec- tion with the R-rune, that there is the further possibility of a link with Mithraic and other traditions of classical antiquity. This is the line taken by Agrell — though he is entirely at one with other interpreters in emphasising the significance of the sun-chariot with its four horses (the *quadriga*): the 'number' of the R-rune in Agrell's system is four.[32]

There are of course a number of other runes
which are interpreted in *Salomon and Saturn*, but I
do not have time to deal with each of them separately. In every case we are, I believe, dealing
with a tenacious tradition which ascribed to each
of the runes a particular power, brought to bear
on a text which, in the eyes of the Christian
Anglo-Saxon, was itself a source of divine protection. It is a moot point whether the author of
the runic part of the dialogues was well versed in
Latin; perhaps he was not. Even were Latin not
known, the Latin words would be regarded (on a
pattern well known from elsewhere in the history
of religion) as being especially powerful, and
therefore to be treated with extreme care. The
vernacular is, of course, never an adequate sub-
stitute for the hieratic language -- a psychological principle which the Roman Catholic Church
seems now lamentably to have forgotten. Of course
in the early days of the Christian Church in this
land, the *Pater Noster* was, with the *Credo*, obli-
gatory learning for the Christian: '...the foundation of faith, the first means to salvation...the
chief and ready shield against temptation and
danger.'[33] Mostly against danger!

What a pity it is, then, that linguistic commentators on *Salomon and Saturn* should be so
easily satisfied as to state baldly, as Menner
does, that 'The use of the runic letters of the
Pater Noster in Poem I is simply a transformation
of the inherited power of Solomon's magical ring
and magical prayers.'[34] In fact the runic usage
is, as I hope I have managed to show, not *simply*
anything, but on the contrary, a complex inter-
weaving of impulses coming from a number of different sources. The inherited power of Solomon's
ring and prayers may have something to do with
this pattern; but I feel it has not a great deal
to do with it.

There remains for me to say a very few words

about the subsequent use of the *Pater Noster* in the Nordic setting — again a subject which of itself forms a fascinating study, and which I can only hint at in this context.

The magical or semi-magical use of palindromes and acrostics in the religious underworld of the middle ages is as evident in the North as elsewhere in Europe. A formula such as *ablanatanalba*, for instance, is to be found in Denmark by the 4th century. But of course the most famous of such formulae is that which has most directly to do with our subject, viz., the SATOR-AREPO:

```
S A T O R
A R E P O
T E N E T
O P E R A
R O T A S
```

Much thought and not a little ingenuity has been spent in trying in later years to find out exactly what this formula may have 'meant'.[35] The results are sometimes ludicrous: what does it help to be informed that the sentence means 'Arepo the sower holds the wheels with difficulty' — other than perhaps conjuring up a helpful picture of an inebriated peasant trying to drive in a straight line? It is perhaps a little more illuminating to learn that the words were the names of the five wounds of Jesus. But in reality the formula need not have meant anything. It was a powerful invocation of the power of the Pater Noster, together with the A and O — Latinised first and last letters of the Greek alphabet. To go beyond this and affirm that SATOR = SA(LVA)TOR and that the other word AREPO = A + R(EX) + E(T) + P(ATER) + O is really not necessary. To be sure, we have moved on a little from the runic symbolism, but the emphasis is unmistakeable.

We may, too, move on from there to other usages of the SATOR-AREPO, though this is not a subject

to which I can devote attention. There is one
point only which I consider worthy of mention. As
an all-purpose formula for both black and white
magic, based so obviously on the *Pater Noster*, one
would have thought that the formula would have, as
it were, fallen on God's side in the great war
over man's soul. But no. Three later names in
Swedish for this formula are 'Fans fyrkant' (the
devil's square), 'Djävulen's Latin' (the devil's
Latin) or 'Hin håles latin' (Old Nick's Latin).
Is it not odd that the sacred letters, which were
once believed to be so powerful as symbols that
the Devil could not stand for one moment under
their onslaught, have now been rearranged in such
a way as to change allegiance altogether?

The reason I believe is to be found mainly in
the rather equivocal relationship in which formulae of power must have stood to the ecclesiastical authorities and the means of grace. Before
the Reformation, these formulae might continue to
survive more or less as part of the main stream of
powerful tradition. But after the Reformation, the
formulae accompanied the runes into the religious
underworld, where on the whole they have lived —
or shall we say existed — ever since.

4. ICONS AS SYMBOLS OF POWER

Venetia Newall

ICONS, THOSE BEAUTIFUL religious paintings,
strange to us but central to the worship of the
Orthodox church, have throughout the centuries
been invested with mysterious powers by those who
prayed to them. For the Orthodox they are closely
linked with the process of prayer [Hecker, 25],
but they are much more than pious aids to con-
centration [Hastings, III.428]. They are symbols
of power: the power of the holy scenes and person-
ages represented in them; power which is enriched
in various ways which we shall be considering —
their placement and ornamentation, their role in
ecclesiastical and secular life, the traditional
style of execution, and the preparations made by
the painters themselves. For the Orthodox Christian an icon is equivalent to the Gospels and the
Cross [French, 133; Ouspensky, 32]; it has been
described as 'the chief visible manifestation of
religious thought' [Hare, 25]. The link between
the icon and what it depicts is established by the
Church. In other words, an icon does not become a
true icon until a priest has blessed it [French,
133, Wallace, 104].

The iconoclast* controversy, which split the
early church, concerned the nature of icons: were
they or were they not idols? It began in the reign
of Pope Leo II [682-683 A.D.] and continued until
843 A.D. when the usage of icons was formally
restored and the Church officially announced that
representations of Christ and the saints contained
'a spark of the divine energy and...their con-
templation was beneficial to the soul' [Grabar, 26].
The 7th Ecumenical Council of 787 A.D., better
known as the 2nd Council of Nicaea, decreed that
icons should be venerated in the same manner as

* Iconoclast: Icon (= image) Klastes (= breaker)

61

the Cross and the Gospels [Ouspensky, 32]. This decision was proclaimed in 843 A.D. as the triumph of Orthodoxy and observed on the 1st Sunday in Lent as Orthodoxy Sunday [Ouspensky, 33; Ware, 39; Bréhier, 173].

The Orthodox response to charges of idolatry runs something like this: the icon is not an idol but a symbol [Ware, 40]. It underlines the doctrine of the incarnation by depicting God made Man [Ware, 41]. The iconoclasts in their attitude tended to separate spirit from matter, whereas the doctrine of Salvation included the whole of creation, material as well as spiritual. Thus icons do not set out to imitate Nature but rather to show both man and creation transfigured [Zernov, 276; Ware, 239]. This is based on *Revelation* xxi. 1: 'Then I saw a new heaven and a new earth; for the first heaven and the first earth had passed away'. Broadly speaking they depict the spiritual breaking in upon the world of the senses [French, 150]. Those persons represented give to the icon its sacred character and the saints are shown as ascetics: their deprived bodies contrasting with radiant faces and robes, they represent the achievement of control over matter.

The earliest surviving icons, which mostly occur in or near Egypt, date from the late 5th or early 6th century [French, 51] and are thought to derive from Egyptian funerary portraits painted on wood and fixed to the shroud of the mummy [Wild, 3; French, 130; Meer and Mohrmann, 163]. The art was developed in Byzantium and spread to Italy, the Balkans, and Russia, which became the spiritual inheritor of Orthodoxy after the fall of Constantinople in 1453 [Hare, 31; Wild, 4]. Throughout its history the style has been a peculiarly strict one. This is not only for the sake of pure conservatism; it is an essential part of the icon preparation process. The icon painter is not called upon to exercise his originality. As a

62

leading, presumably agnostic, art critic expressed
it recently, he is performing a magical act, and
'if he strayed too far from the accepted model,
then perhaps the magic would not happen.' [Lucie-
Smith, *The Times*, Dec 7, 1965]. The icon is part
of a continuing tradition which reflects the
thinking of the church and scenes of events regarded as historically correct and accurately depicted have persisted as iconographic types, in
some cases for more than a thousand years [Lasar-
eff and Demus, 21].

In 1551 the Council of the Hundred Chapters, a
Russian ecclesiastical body convened in the reign
of Tsar Ivan the Terrible, decreed that: 'The
holy and venerable icons, conformable to divine
rules, must reproduce the image of God, his likeness, and be faithful to the consecrated type.
[According to the rules] one will paint the image
of God, of the Most Pure Mother of God and that of
all the intercessor saints...the painters will reproduce the ancient models. In nothing will the
painters follow their own fancy.' [Hamilton, 101].
Gerhard relates this synod to the Fall of Constantinople in 1453 when, as he puts it, 'people were
looking for a new foundation, new principles on
which to build' [Gerhard, 176].

After the Great Fire of Moscow burnt numerous
churches and their contents Ivan the Terrible
[1533-84] established official icon workshops and
imported numbers of artists, especially from Germany and Italy. A century later they had been
joined by Poles, Jews, Greeks, Swedes, Tartars and
Armenians [Hare, 34]. The hierarchy of the church
was strongly opposed to outside innovators however,
and in 1655 the Patriarch Nikon held a service of
condemnation at the Cathedral of the Dormition in
the Kremlin, when he excommunicated not only those
who had painted in a Western rather than a traditional manner, but even those who displayed such
icons in their homes [Hare, 35]. After showing

63

some examples to the congregation, he smashed them
to pieces on the stone floor of the cathedral.
They were then to be publicly burnt, but the Tsar,
who was in the congregation, remonstrated with him
and the fragments were buried instead [Hare, 35].
The same Patriarch Nikon also seized untraditional
Western icons from private homes, even from high
dignitaries of State. The eyes were pierced and in
this condition the offending icons were paraded
through the streets of Moscow.

Archpriest Avvakum went a stage further and declared that all icons of holy figures should represent them as thin and emaciated. Those that did
not were 'of the Devil': 'By God's will much un-
seemly foreign painting has spread over our
Russian land. They paint the image of our Saviour
Emmanuel with a puffy face, and red lips, curly
hair, fat arms and muscles, and stout legs and
thighs. And all this is done for carnal reasons,
because the heretics love sensuality and do not
care for higher things.' [Hamilton, 157].

The tradition of depicting saints as taller
than ordinary people is intended to underline the
difference between the material and celestial
worlds [T.Talbot Rice, *Concise History*, 34] and
size is often proportionate to ideological importance. We may also compare the ancient Slav concept
of their pagan gods as 'taller than the skies'
[Onasch, 357-8].

Colour schemes also fell under traditional
practice. Hues which had originally been clear and
brilliant, but which darkened with the passing of
time, were taken as sacrosanct in their changed
form and scrupulously adhered to in later centuries. But if the faces were sometimes dark and
gaunt the background shimmered, for it symbolised
the shining glory of heaven, and for this reason
it was usually executed in gold leaf over a coat-
ing of red wine. It had a special name 'svet',
which means light [T.Talbot Rice, *Russian Icons*, 24].

64

There were various painters' manuals, called
Podlinniki in Russian, in which the many rules
were gathered together. One of the best known was
The Painters Book of Mount Athos, named after the
famous Greek promontory* where about 20 Orthodox
monasteries are housed. It contains instructions
on the use of colour, presentation, and details of
style. Very little indeed is left to fancy [Wild,
8-9]. So important is this adherence to traditional style that an icon correctly copied is said to
possess as much efficacy as the original [Lucie
Smith, *The Times*].

The icon painters, who were obliged to follow
these rules, carried a heavy burden of respons-
ibility. They had to be practising Christians, who
prepared themselves for their work by the sacra-
ments of Confession and Holy Communion [Ware, 214].
A letter addressed to the Tsar Alexis and Patriarch Nikon, dated 1648, describes the preparations
made at Mount Athos preparatory to painting a copy
of an icon: 'In response to your Majesty's will
and the word from the saintly Lord Archimandrite
Nikon of the new Spassov monastery, I, on my
arrival into our monastery gathered our whole
fraternity of three hundred and sixty-five breth-
ren for much prayer and song, lasting from evening
until sunrise. We blessed water with holy relics
(that is, bodily remains of dead saints) and
poured this holy water over the sacred miracle-
working icon of the blessed God-bearer, the old
Portaitess; we collected this water into a great
basin and again and again poured it over the new
icon, made of cedar wood. Then we gathered this
water into a basin and zealously celebrated divine
and holy mass. After the holy mass we gave this
holy water and the holy relics to the icon painter,
the Reverend Friar and Holy Father, Lord Yamblik-
hon Romanov, in order that he, after mixing the

* A peninsula off the coast of N.E. Greece.

holy water with the relics and the colours, might
paint the holy and blessed icon, in order that the
panel and the colours be joined with the holy
water and the relics. And in painting this holy
icon, he partook of food only on Saturdays and
Sundays and completed it in great silence with joy
and vigilance' [Hecker, 24-5; Dawkins, 270]. The
account goes on to say that during the painting of
the icon the Father Superior of the Monastery and
the 365 monks prayed all night from dusk to dawn
twice a week and said mass daily until the icon
was finished; this took about 2 weeks.

If the icon was to be satisfactory and effective, the man who painted it must be truly
righteous and God-fearing. The Council of the
Hundred Chapters decreed (1551): 'The painter
should be filled with humility, meekness and piety;
he should shun frivolous talk and amusement. He
must be peaceable by nature and know no envy. He
must neither drink, nor rob, nor steal. Above all,
he should be extemely careful to safeguard his
spiritual and physical purity. If he is unable to
live in chastity, he should take a wife and marry
according to the law. He should pay numerous
visits to his spiritual fathers and inform them
about his way of life and, in keeping with their
commands and instructions, fast and pray, culti-
vate purity and modesty and keep all shamelessness
and turbulence far from him.' [Gerhard, 177]. The
bishops and priests were instructed to ensure that
the painter lived a suitable worthy life [Hamilton,
101]. This would have presented no problem in
medieval times, when the artists were usuallly
monks, and even later when icon painting became a
family skill handed down from father to son, men
who did their best to live a life in keeping with
their sacred work. Tamara Talbot Rice has compared
them to actors in the Oberammergau Passion Play
who try, as far as possible, to live like the
protagonist they represent in the sacred drama

[T.Talbot Rice, *Russian Icons*, 10-11]. One could
make a closer comparison with the Jewish scribe,
whose task it was to write the scrolls of the law.
The exact manner in which it had to be done was
carefully laid down, even to the spacing between
letters, words and lines, so that the style has
remained virtually unchanged for two thousand
years. Writing the scroll was regarded as a sacred
task and the scribe wore religious objects while
he worked, the prayer shawl and phylacteries. He
had to use the best ink, the finest quill pen and
make every effort to avoid errors. Above all he
had to be pious 'clean of hand and thought and
filled with devotion to God' [Idelsohn, 88-9;
Ausubel, 478-9]. One assumes that these scribes
and the early icon painters would have voluntarily
and cheerfully undertaken these onerous duties.
But in the official icon workshops of 16th century Russia and later, many craftsmen must have
laboured unhappily under the exhortations to live
modestly, not to quarrel or drink overmuch alcohol
and so on [Hare, 33].

According to traditional belief the icon painters were divinely inspired [Wallace, 104]. When
the saintly Alipy lay dying, his patron badgered
him to finish an uncompleted icon. He had no
strength to continue the task, but an angel descended from heaven, did the work, hung the icon
in position and led the venerable master to paradise. Alipy, an 11th century monk, was responsible for some of the work in the Uspenski Church
of Kiev [Gerhard, 120-1]. Such legends are common
[cf. Dawkins, 215-6]. The prototype of the icon
painter is St Luke, the patron saint of artists,
who is said to have painted various portraits of
the Virgin [Ferguson, 131, 178; Wild, 3].

There are various ways of arranging icons. One
of the best known, which first evolved in Russia,
is the iconostasis [Wild, 7], the wall of pictures
which separates the altar from the main body of

the church, and is related to the chancel screen
of the West. Originally this demarcation was indicated by a low marble wall in Byzantine churches,
and this developed into an arcade. Icons were
fixed to the columns, and as they were often
bulky and difficult to move, a complete wall of
pictures arranged in a special order gradually
developed. This was in the early 14th century
[T.Talbot Rice, *Russian Icons*, 10, 68; Hamilton,
66; Bunt, 83]. It is the main focus of attention
in an Orthodox church and Tamara Talbot Rice be-
lieves that it may have first arisen in the
thickly forested Novgorod region, where the people
were skilled in wood carving [T.Talbot Rice,
Russian Icons, 68].

The iconostasis has a central door and two
side ones. The main entrance usually has over it a
deësis, a group of 3 icons consisting of Christ
the Pantocrator or Ruler of the Universe, flanked
by the Virgin and John the Baptist. These doors
separate the congregation from the holy area and
only clergy and the Tsar on the occasion of his
coronation are permitted to use it. Lay men may
use the side doors, but never women [Wild, 44].
The iconostasis has been described as the gateway
to the heavenly places [Information from Fr.Hayes]
and an indication of its importance as a symbol
and focus of religious power and strength is perhaps suggested by the perverse Soviet recognition
[Spring 1923 and 4 years after] of the only Orthodox Church leader — Antonin, Bishop of Narva — who
had called for the elimination of the iconostasis
[Bourdeaux, 28]. This was in the early 1920s.

Individual icons were also placed in other
parts of the church to be kissed and venerated. In
Moldavia, a Rumanian province, it was quite usual
to have a secret chamber in the church ceiling
where ecclesiastical treasure was kept, the entrance concealed by an icon. No doubt the presence
of the sacred object was also intended to deter

68

any would-be thief [Personal observations, Moldo-
viţa 1963]. It is interesting to note in this connection that in Constantinople portraits of heretics, Arius [260-336] for example, were used to
decorate the floors of the latrines [Gerhard, 23].

In pre-revolutionary Russia there were icons in
all the public buildings and vehicles — shops,
railways, barracks, buses and cars [Ware, 261;
French, 154-5]. Here is Gogol, describing a typi-
cal country tavern of 19th century Russia in *Dead
Souls* [1837]: 'The room contained all those old
friends whom it is the lot of everyone to meet in
small wooden taverns...a frost-rimed samovar,
smoothly scraped pine-wood walls, a three cornered
cupboard with tea-pots and cups in one corner,
gilt porcelain eggs dangling on blue and red
ribbons in front of the icons...and...bundles of
fragrant herbs and cloves in the vicinity of the
icons, all so dried up that anyone attempting to
smell them could only sneeze' [Gogol, 70].

The icons mentioned here were a feature of
every Orthodox household and visitors would stand
before them, bowing and crossing themselves, before greeting their host [Iswolsky, 161]. There
was a correct position for them in the room
[French, 132] in the eastern corner [Iswolsky,
160-1], also described as the inner right-hand
corner [T.Talbot Rice, *Russian Icons*, 10] and
known as the Red Corner, for red in Old Slavonic
signified beautiful, a significance which has been
taken up and effectively used by the Soviets as
the colour of revolution. In the houses of the
well-to-do, a special room was set apart as an
oratory with lamps burning in front of the icons
[Kondakov, 34; Iswolsky, 160-1]. These home
shrines possessed the dual function of ensuring a
blessing upon the family and warding off evil
[Wild, 6; Wallace, 106]. They were often beautifully decorated with ceremonial white towels,
which could be embroidered [Kondakov, 38]. Such

festive towels were sometimes draped above the
icon as they were also occasionally on wayside
crosses and the branches of neighbouring trees.
This could indicate the Christianisation of a
pagan votive offering to sacred trees [Bunt, 196].
In Rumania the custom was explained by saying that
an icon was too sacred to be touched by hand, and
in Russia special icons were veiled with silk
curtains 'against the doings of everyday life'
[Kondakov, 34; Bunt, 184]. A study of pre-war Bulgarian village life describes how each home had a
small wooden iconostasis in the east or southeast
corner of the room, and if some calamity befell
the household they obtained an icon of the saint
whose day it was, added it to their iconostasis,
sprinkled the house with holy water, and did no
work on that day ever after [Sanders, 24]. At
Christmas in the same country the censor from the
iconostasis was carried round the house, to each
room, and out to the animals in their stalls to
bring good luck [Sanders, 106].

Icons were associated with every stage of human
development: schools, regiments, clubs, prisons,
and other social groups all possessed their own
icons [French, 132]. There were also icons of a
more personal nature. Orthodox Christians customarily had a patron saint whom they were named
after and a new-born baby would be presented with
a birth icon of that particular holy person [Kon-
dakov, 34]. In the Middle Ages each member of the
congregation had his own icon which hung in the
church and to which he prayed. If anyone prayed to
someone else's icon an unpleasant situation was
liable to develop, for the owner believed that
this was 'stealing grace' from the holy picture
[Hecker, 25].

Some people carried a miniature of their patron
saint about in their pocket. They might hang one
in the bedroom and after death the family placed
one in church as a commemorative act [Wallace, 110].

These coffin or funerary icons were placed on the corpse for the last rites and kissed as a final mark of respect for the dead in Bulgaria [Sanders, 38; Kondakov, 34].

Another important category of icon are those which are carried in procession [D.Talbot Rice, 85; Kondakov, 80], like the miraculous icon of the Virgin at Panaghia Xenia Monastery, on Mount Othrys in Thessaly, which is taken round the fields in summer to keep off the plagues of locusts [Dawkins, 346]. The custom is thought to have evolved from a tradition of the Byzantine emperors who had their portraits carried in procession [Gerhard, 26]. Banner icons are called *Prapure* in Rumania, where it was supposed until the 19th century that removing the icon from a procession invoking rain would nullify the purpose of the operation [Information supplied by Professor Vulcănescu]. One of these icons would be placed in front of a house where there had been a recent death, to protect the family. Anyone daring to steal it would find that his aged relatives were prevented from dying [Information supplied by Professor Vulcănescu].

It was more usual, throughout the Orthodox countries, to make a votive offering to the icons. Athenian women used to dedicate a new spindle to the family icons on the Monday of St Thomas, that is Monday week following Easter, so that it came to be known as the Spindle Resurrection [Megas, 113]. Albanians offered the icon a piece of New Year cake [Spicer, 3], and the saw of a sword fish hangs before an icon of the Virgin at Kykko, a thank-offering from a Cypriot sailor for rescue from drowning [Gunnis, 305]. There is a bronze arm in front of the same icon. The story goes that a sacrilegious Turk tried to light his cigarette at the icon lamp, but the portrait of the Virgin stopped him in the act and changed the arm into bronze [Gunnis, 305]. This aetiological legend

purports to explain the presence of a very usual
votive item before an icon. Shapes representing
different parts of the body which have experienced
miraculous cures are often utilised in this way.
On a visit to Serbia, Cecil Stewart saw fingers,
hearts and legs in silver applied to the surface
of different icons. He also noted strings of them
hanging round specially venerated pictures
[Stewart, 59]. Olive Chapman, calling at the
Cypriot Monastery of St Andrew on the Carpas Pen-
ninsula, saw gifts attached to the banners near
the iconostasis. There was jewellery, gold and
silver necklaces and bracelets, and more humble
offerings like a child's celluloid toy. There were
silver models of eyes and noses, as well as arms
and legs. She writes: 'Most curious of all was the
row of nude wax male and female figures, standing
stiffly upright like dolls in wooden cases, at the
back of the church. They varied from two to four
feet in height, and I was told that each represented the soul of a man or woman who had been
cured by St Andrew. Some of them were very old;
others had been presented quite recently. I
noticed for instance, the model of a man [who] had
caused himself to be modelled in a modern coat and
trousers. Of all the figures, however, his was the
only one that was clothed. Another recent acqui-
sition was a crude model of a female, about three
feet high. The donor, a beautiful girl from
Nicosia, evidently wishing for her likeness to be
seen, had had an enlarged photograph of her head
stuck on to the waxen body of the doll. Beneath
was written her name and that of the photographer.
The models were all of human beings except one,
which represented a small animal, probably a mule'
[Chapman, 85-6].

Occasionally coins are offered. In the church
of the skete of St Anne on Mount Athos there is a
famous icon of the saint and a 19th century German
visitor describes how he was told to hold out a

coin and it was attracted towards the picture as
if by a magnet [Dawkins, 216]. In Rumania icons of
St Mennas were believed to attract silver coins —
a sign not of greed but of divine power. Worship-
pers prayed and made the sign of the cross with
the coin. If the icon attracted it magnetically,
it was a sign that the prayer would be answered
[Information from Professor Vulcănescu]. A coin
adhering to an icon as an offering reflects the
Middle Eastern custom of sticking a coin to a
person's face as a mark of approval [Dawkins, 217].
In Greece it was used as a test to see if one's
wishes would come true: if the coin stuck to the
icon, all would be well. But if it fell, disap-
pointment was in store. The church of St Paraskeve
at Chalcis was noted for the practice of this
custom on July 25. The writer of a 19th century
book on Greece observes that the church: 'is
largely frequented by those whose soberer reason
is temporarily deranged by the passion of love'
[Rodd, 164]. It has been suggested [Lawson, 301]
that the observance is related to the pagan custom
of covering venerated statues with gold and silver
foil by way of a thank-offering. One sees the connection more obviously in the tradition of partially covering an icon with repoussé metalwork,
often of silver, and perhaps decorated with jewels
or enamel [Stewart, 59; French, 130], a habit
which originated as a gift of thanks for miraculous cures and other favours granted [Gerhard, 26].

With the passing of time the details were lost
as to the origins of some of the older icons and
they received a miraculous pedigree. Some of the
Virgin, as we have seen, were attributed to St
Luke. Others, especially if they were well-known,
were said to be *nerukotvornii* — not made by human
hands [Bunt, 109]. An important and early example
of this type is the Sacred Face, called in the
West 'The Vernicle', where it derives from the
legend of St Veronica. According to the Apocryphal

Gospel of Nicodemus, St Veronica wiped the sweat from Christ's face as He walked to Calvary and the imprint of His features was left on the cloth [Attwater, *Dic. of Saints*, 334-5; Ferguson, 146]. A 5th century Eastern legend states that the Saviour pressed a cloth to his face and sent it to Abgar, the ailing King of Edessa* [179-214 A.D.] and he was healed [Wild, 44; Ouspensky, 69-70]. It was afterwards taken to Constantinople and was destroyed when the city fell to the crusaders in 1204 [Gerhard, 84]. A fresco in a Moldavian monastery shows the 7th century Siege of Constantinople, when the city was saved from the Avars and the Persians by display of an icon of the Virgin and of the Sacred Face [Grabar-Oprescu, 14]. It was this last icon which the 7th Ecumenical Council [787 A.D.] decreed should be specially venerated on Orthodoxy Sunday when the victory over the iconoclasts is celebrated [Ouspensky, 69-7)].

Christ the Pantocrator, or Ruler of the Universe, is normally represented holding an open Bible, his right hand raised in blessing, but in the dome of St Sophia at Novgorod the fingers of the hand are closed. There is a legend that, when the figure was painted, a voice from the heavens told the artist to paint the right hand thus 'for in this, my right hand, I hold Novgorod'. When the hand opened, Novgorod would perish. This is evidently another aetiological legend accounting for the hand being painted in this unusual manner [Fedotov, 360-1; Kondakov, 94].

An icon of the Saviour, set up by Constantine in the Brass Market of Constantinople, features in a remarkable legend of conversion, or perhaps one might term it religious propaganda. A 7th century merchant borrows money from a Jew named Abraham, using the icon as guarantor. He raises the repay-

* Edessa is the modern town of Urfa in Turkey.

ment overseas and sends it to Abraham, who receives it but lies to the merchant on his return as a test of his faith. The merchant takes Abraham before the icon and lightning flashes from it as a sign, while the merchant's cargo of tin and lead is changed to silver. The Jew is thereupon baptised and becomes a priest, and the merchant enters a monastic order [Dawkins, 210]. An interesting feature of this highly improbable tale is the underlying assumption that a Jew would regard an icon as a symbol of power. Above the Spassky Gate into the Kremlin was an icon of Christ, said to have been placed there in 1626, and every man passing beneath it was compelled by Imperial decree to uncover his head [Grove, 51-2].

After the Saviour, the most important iconographic subject is the Virgin, known in the Eastern Church as the Mother of God. There are many different types and emphasis is placed, not on her Virginity, but on the concept of divine motherhood [Fedotov. I. 376]. In Rumania religious folk believed she was emblematic of Summer, the fruitful time of year, and her icon was an essential part of a young bride's dowry, for it represented fecundity [Irimie-Focşa, 15].

Tradition says that various icons of the Virgin were painted by St Luke and indeed that he was responsible for producing the first [Wild, 3; French, 134]. This legend is attached to the famous icon of Our Lady of Vladimir, one of the most ancient, and the most lovely, icons in Russia. He completed it while the Mother of God was still alive and when she was shown it she prophesied 'All generations shall call me blessed' [Luke. i. 48] for 'with this image is my grace and power' [Ouspensky, 94]. Utilised at the coronation of the Tsars and the consecration of the Patriarchs until the Revolution, it enjoyed a special place in the hearts of the Russian people. It was their most sacred treasure and through its association with

the major events of Russian history came to be regarded as a national palladium, preserving the
people from harm [Ouspensky, 94; Hamilton, 70]. It
was painted in Constantinople for Prince Izyaslav
of Kiev in about 1132 and for political reasons
Prince Andrew Bogolyubski later took it to
Vladimir, the city from which it derives its name.
It is said that the horses transporting the icon
to Rostov would not move once they had reached
Vladimir. Bogolyubski was thus enabled to set up
his central government in a new area, Vladimir,
out of reach from the powerful princes of Rostov
[Hamilton, 70]. Here the miraculous icon provides
supernatural sanction for political action. Each
occasion when the icon was moved elsewhere is recorded in the Chronicles of Russia [Ouspensky, 94].
Its history is not one of unqualified success:
when the Tartars sacked Vladimir in 1237 they removed all the gold and jewels from the frame of
the icon [Hamilton, 70; Hecker, 22]. Indeed
Ainalov suggests that, even at this stage, following the great conflagration of 1185, a copy may
have been in use [Gerhard, 76-9]. These events do
not seem to have affected the reputation of the
painting and in 1395, when Tamerlane advanced towards Moscow, the icon was borrowed from Vladimir
and carried to Moscow [T.Talbot Rice, *Russian
Icons*, 29], where great kneeling crowds lined the
route, crying 'Mother of God! Save the Russian
land!' When the icon reached Moscow, Tamerlane,
asleep in his tent,is said to have seen a vision
of a lofty mountain moving towards him. A great
company of saints bearing golden crosiers descended the slopes, and a woman surrounded with thou-
sands of warriors hovered above them, illumined
by shining light. Tamerlane summoned his advisers
to interpret what he had seen, and was told that
the woman was the Mother of the Christians' God
and their protector, who would preserve them from
his invading armies. [Hecker, 21-3].

76

The fact that Tamerlane then withdrew, for whatever reason, is a historic fact and the city's miraculous deliverance was ascribed to the powers of the icon. The commemoration of this icon took place 3 times a year, all on dates linked with the deliverance of Moscow from the Tartars: August 26, 1395, June 23, 1480, and May 21, when the icon was renewed in 1514 and the Tartars repelled in 1521 [Ouspensky, 94]. Later it encouraged the troops who saved Moscow from the Poles in 1612: 'It is better for us to die than to deliver the image of the immaculate Mother of God of Vladimir to desecration' [Ouspensky, 94].

Many of the famous Russian icons have a notable war history [Hecker, 21] and ruling princes were accustomed to seizing icons from elsewhere if they lacked them, to obtain their supernatural protective powers in battle [Hecker, 21]. There is no doubt that such a trophy would also have been very good for the morale of the troops. Another famous Russian icon, the Virgin of the Don, is linked with the first defeat of the Tartars at the Battle of Kulikovo in 1380 [Onasch, 383-4; Hamilton, 85], and the Virgin of Smolensk, one of those attributed to the hand of St Luke, inspired the Russian troops to hold out against the armies of Napoleon in 1812. Here is Tolstoy's description in *War and Peace*: 'Following the battalion that marched along the dusty road, came priests in their vestments...Behind them soldiers and officers bore a large dark-faced icon with an embossed metal cover. This was the icon that had been brought from Smolensk and had since accompanied the army. Behind, before, and on both sides, crowds of militiamen with bared heads, walked, ran, and bowed to the ground.

At the summit of the hill they stopped with the icon; the men who had been holding it up by the linen bands attached to it were relieved by others, the chanters relit their censers and service began.

The hot rays of the sun beat down vertically, and
a fresh soft wind played with the hair of the
bared heads and with the ribbons decorating the
icon...An immense crowd of bareheaded officers,
soldiers and militiamen surrounded the icon...A
bald general with a St George's Cross on his neck
stood just behind the priest's back, and without
crossing himself (he was evidently a German)
patiently awaited the end of the service, which he
considered it necessary to hear to the end, probably to arouse the patriotism of the Russian
people...Standing among the crowd of peasants,
Pierre recognised several acquaintances...but did
not look at them — his whole attention was ab-
sorbed in watching the serious expression on the
faces of the crowd of soldiers and militiamen who
were all gazing eagerly at the icon.' [Tolstoy. X.
470-472].

Our Lady of Kazan, one of the types which sometimes occur on Russian porcelain Easter eggs, encouraged the troops in 1612 against the Poles, and
200 years later against the armies of Napoleon
[Ouspensky, 88]. A young girl dreamed persistently
that the Virgin had indicated to her the site
where the icon was buried, so she and her mother
found it and placed it in the cathedral. It is of
some interest here that this event took place in
1579 at Kazan, the capital of a Tartar Khanat
[Ouspensky, 88].

The Virgin of the Sign, called Znamenie, the
Russian for 'sign', is another battle icon, associated with the victory in 1169 of the people of
Novgorod, following a siege by the armies of Suzdal,
the two city states being rival powers. Here again,
the Virgin is the palladium of the city. When the
icon is displayed on the city walls, the Suzdalians shoot arrows at it, whereupon the image turns
away weeping and the tears are gathered up by the
archbishop in his stole. The 15th century icon of
The Fight Between the Suzdalians and the Novgorod-

ians is of particular interest because it illustrates in an icon the wonder-working powers of
another icon. It is also said to be the earliest
icon which specifically deals with an event in
Russian history. When the Novgorodians hasten to
avenge the sacrilege, their armies are depicted
with four popular battle saints riding in the van-
guard: St Boris, St George, St Gleb and Alexander
Nevsky. A warrior angel hovers overhead [Hamilton,
90; Onasch, 364-5]. The Virgin of the Sign is here
a symbol of Novgorod, the powerful city state
[Onasch, 364-5]. The legend, a Russian version of
the defence of Constantinople, was written by the
15th century Serbian author, Vitas Pachomij Logo-
fit [Onasch, 364].

In the Intercession of the Virgin, a type of
the Virgin of Shelter and Refuge, her veil appears
above the people as a symbolic spiritual shelter.
Sometimes she holds it herself and sometimes it is
supported by two angels. From an early date the
Church of the Blachernae in Constantinople contained the veil or omophorion of the Virgin, which
Andrew, the Fool in Christ [D. 936 A.D.] saw there
in a vision, spread over the people and shimmering
in the air [Hamilton, 91-2; Onasch, 344-5]. The
Virgin as Intercessor is a popular subject for
Russian icons. It dates back to the Saracen invasion of the Greek Empire in the 10th century and
flourished in Russia during the invasions of the
Tartar Mongols. It has been suggested that there
may be a derivation here from a pre-Christian protective rite associated with the cult of the
mother goddess [Onasch, 344-5].

The concept of a battle icon is one which takes
many and varied forms. It could be bestowed on an
individual as a protective amulet, its power
strengthened by the loving concern of the giver
for the wearer's personal safety. Readers of *War
and Peace* will remember the famous passage when
Princess Mary says goodbye to her agnostic brother

79

Prince Andrew, who is leaving for the Napoleonic Wars: 'Andrew, I bless you with this icon and you must promise me you will never take it off... Against your will He will save and have mercy on you and bring you to Himself, for in Him alone is truth and peace," said she in a voice trembling with emotion, solemnly holding up in both hands before her brother a small, oval, antique, dark-faced icon of the Saviour in a gold setting, on a finely wrought silver chain. She crossed herself, kissed the icon, and handed it to Andrew.' [Tolstoy. I. 134].

As the pre-revolution religious period of Russian history began to draw to its close, there was a final and striking example of faith in a battle icon. During the Russian-Japanese War of 1904-05, the last Tsar Nicholas II, a deeply religious man, sent a supply train to the front where the Russian troops, woefully short of ammunition, were being massacred by the Japanese because they had nothing with which to repel them. The officer in charge eagerly met the train only to discover, to his dismay, that the train contained, not ammunition, but a consignment of icons of the Holy Seraphim of Sarov, one for each soldier, a personal gift from the Tsar. The son of this officer comments in his Memoirs: 'The Tsar was a firm believer in the power of the Seraphim of Sarov, who had been recently canonised on his own Imperial decree; it was through the intervention of this saint that the Tsaritsa had at last been blessed with a son, the heir to the throne...A few miles away Russian soldiers were being massacred by the Japs because they had no ammunition to hold the Orientals at bay. And now, to protect them, they were sent icons. It was not without point that...General Dragomirov had said that the Japanese fought with cannons and the Russians with icons' [Sava, 121].

During the Second World War the Italians in-

vaded Greece and before they were repulsed everyone prayed to the icon of Tenos. The subsequent
victory was regarded as a miracle [Told to the
author; Tenos, August 1960]. Tenos, described as
the Lourdes of the Orthodox faith, attracts pilgrims twice in the year from all over the Greek
world, and the fact that the Greek cruiser *Elli*
was torpedoed during the celebrations in 1940 did
not apparently shake confidence in its wondrous
powers. Had it done so, its subsequent success in
countering the Italian invasion would doubtless
have restored the faith of any waverers, since it
was supposed that the Italians were responsible
for the disaster. The icon, the Holy Virgin of the
Annunciation, is celebrated on two of her feasts:
the Annunciation (March 25) and the Dormition
(August 15). It may be described as the palladium
of the Greek people, for it was discovered hidden
in the ground, the result of a miraculous dream,
in the year 1821, when the Greek War of Independ-
ence was declared, on the Feast of the Annunciation [Hamilton, *Greek Saints*, 77ff]. The Virgin,
who appeared in the dream, commanded that a church
should be built on the place where the icon was
found, a usual explanation given for the foundation of numerous Greek churches [Hamilton, *Greek
Saints*, 77]. Said to have been painted by St Luke,
it is credited with curative powers. It is believed to have healed the inhabitants of Tenos
when they were suffering from the plague [Hamilton,
Greek Saints, 78], and in 1964,when King Paul of
the Hellenes was dying, Crown Prince Constantine
was despatched in a warship to bring the picture
to his father's bedside: 'for visitation, cure,
and healing.' [*The Times*, March 4, 1964]. It has
been taken to Athens on several other occasions of
national crisis [*Observer*, March 8, 1964]. On August 15, 1960, when I visited Tenos, 35 thousand
Greek pilgrims crowded on to the tiny island, and
the narrow flagged street leading up to the Church

of the Annunciation was crowded with the sick, the
dying, and truly appalling cripples, who lay down
and waited for the sacred icon to be carried over
them. Most of us were obliged to sleep out of
doors as there was insufficient accommodation, and
all the food supplies had run out by the evening.

Another important Greek feast day is May 21st,
dedicated to St Constantine and St Helena, the
Emperor of Constantinople and his revered mother.
Celebrations take place all over Greece and in
Macedonia, in the region of Salonika, Verria,
Drama and Serrai, the Anastenarides, a religious
sect, perform a special dance. The preparatory
ceremonies involve killing a flower-decked bull,
but first the sign of the cross is made over the
creature with an icon of the two saints, which is
hung with bells to ward off evil spirits. The bull
is sacrificed and on the evening of the festival a
bonfire is lit. Each of the Anastenarides takes it
in turn to dance upon the burning embers, barefoot,
and clasping the icons of St Constantine and St
Helena. To remain untouched by the fire is a sign
of personal sanctity, for it is said that: 'The
icon summons only him who is clean' [Megas, 122-5;
Roux, 167-8].

On Mount Athos, the Greek Holy Mountain, one of
the most notable icons is of the Portaitissa, the
Virgin of the Gate, said to have been found washed
up on the beach by the monks of the Georgian monastery of Iviron [Attwater, *Saints of East*, 116].
This is the picture referred to earlier as copied
for Tsar Alexei in 1648. The legend is that in the
time of the iconoclast Emperor Theophilos [829-842
A.D.], a widow living in Nicaea threw the icon
into the sea to save it from the authorities,
crying: 'As thou canst save us from the wrath of
the emperor, so thou canst save thyself from the
danger of the waves.' The icon made its way west-
ward across the waters, floating upright for 70
years, until it reached Athos, preceded by a

82

pillar of fire. It was placed in the monastery
church and three times moved itself to a place
above the entrance gate. A chapel was accordingly
built there and this is how the icon received its
name: the Virgin of the Gate. A Saracen who at-
tacked the icon was converted to Christianity
when he saw that the wound he had made was bleed-
ing [Dawkins, 257ff]. The picture is protectoress
of the Monastery, having announced in a vision:
'I have not come here for you to guard me, but for
me to guard you.'

Such a story of a miraculous voyage to escape
sacrilege is not uncommon. It is paralleled by a
mid 9th century icon of Christ, which crossed the
sea floating upright, from Constantinople to Rome,
bearing a letter, and returned with the answer
[Dawkins, 243]. A version has attached itself to
Our Lady of Good Counsel, one of the most venerated pictures of the Madonna in the West. Now in
the Augustinian church at Genazzano, 30 miles S.E.
of Rome, it is said to have flown there in 1467
from Scutari in Albania, to avoid the Turks. It
was earlier supposed to have arrived miraculously
in Scutari to escape the iconoclasm of previous
centuries and was seen by two pilgrims departing
thence on a white cloud on its final journey
[Dawkins, 243].

[Attwater, *Dic. of Mary*, 97-8]. April 25th is
celebrated in Genazzano as the day of the coming
of the Madonna, when she is said to have arrived
at precisely 4.15 p.m. in the afternoon [Riccardi,
27]. The monks of Crete tell a legend of the Virgin of the Walnut Tree. In the time of the Byzantine Empire the icon hung in a church of Constantinople, but it flew to a monastery near Krasi in
Northern Crete. When it was returned the icon was
fastened to a church column with a chain. But it
flew back to Crete, taking the column with it, and
so was allowed to stay [Dawkins, 212].

Another prominent theme in many of these

legends is the role of the icon as founder of a
church. One of the most curious concerns the Virgin with Three Hands in the Serbian Monastery of
Chiliandari on Mount Athos. The third hand is said
to have assisted with the building of the monastery. The story goes that the painting was originally housed in Serbia itself at the Studnica Monastery. One day there was a fire and the picture
escaped by riding away on a mule, which never stopped till it fell down dead at Chiliandari. Monks
in a neighbouring monastery noticed an unearthly
glow, which was coming from the icon, found it,
and placed it in their iconostasis. During the
night the picture removed itself to the abbot's
choir stall and this happened three times, so ever
since there has not been an abbot at Chiliandari,
because it is the Virgin who is head of the Monastery [Wild, 52]. Here a very charming legend
serves to explain what was evidently an artist's
rough first draft with an extra hand. Dawkins relates the origins of the legend to a period when
the monks were quarrelling as to who should become the new abbot. A variant of the legend describes how the icon was found hanging in a tree.
Such stories, with the accompanying detail of the
shining light are very common. They are related to
the icon of the Virgin of the Burning Bush [Kond-
akov, 38], held to be a type of the Incarnation:
the fire which appeared in the Bush parallels the
Child in the womb of the Virgin [Dawkins, 282].

In Cyprus rain-inducing icons, of which there
are a number, are usually of the Virgin. One of
the most famous, reputedly painted by St Luke, is
in the monastery at Kykko. This icon has been
covered since the 16th century and anyone who
looks at it will meet with a terrible fate [Gunnis,
304]. A monk who disobeyed this was struck down by
a hot blast of air from the icon and was speech-
less for some while after [Hackett, 341]. During a
drought it is taken down from the Monastery and

84

put on a stage facing the direction of the desired
rainfall [D.Talbot Rice, 169]. Other icons of the
Virgin are utilised in different ways by different
villages. At Deftera a service is celebrated in
the dry river bed, and here we may compare the
Rumanian custom, which persisted until the 19th
century, of stealing an icon of the Virgin from a
church and throwing it into the waters of a flowing river to provoke rain; this all had to be done
by a young maiden [Information from Professor
Vulcănescu]. In Athona village it is important to
remove the 16th century icon from the new church
to the ancient Church of the Virgin of Trasha,
where the service is held. At Lythrangomi the
villagers from round about gather for the service.
The priest takes the picture from the iconostasis
at sunset and everyone processes to a Chapel beside the sea where the service is celebrated and
the icon is dipped three times in the water. By
the time it has been returned to the iconostasis
it will have started to rain: this is the local
belief [D.Talbot Rice, 169]. When the Turks occupied Cyprus in 1570, one of their officers rode
past the church where the icon is housed and
slashed a fresco of the Virgin with his sword. It
bled, staining his hand and weapon, and nothing
would remove the blood till he dipped them in the
water of a holy well. This icon is a land owner,
thanks to the bounty of pious parishioners, and it
is said that the Virgin visits her property from
time to time in the guise of a basket of fire
[D.Talbot Rice, 169].

We can see that icons of the Virgin possessed
many and varied functions. Icons of the saints had
more specific roles to play. There are large
numbers of them and it will only be possible to
mention a few of the best loved and the more
bizarre. St Nicholas is a very popular figure.
Customarily represented in the robes of a bishop
[Bunt, 98], his icon is often framed with minature

scenes from his life. This type of biographical icon, *zhiteynie* in Russian [T.Talbot Rice, *Russian Icons*, 18], provides in pictorial form simple object lessons in Christian practice [Wallace, 112], thereby contributing added force and power to the icon. In the West, Nicholas, a 4th century Bishop of Myra in Turkey, whose feast occurs on December 6th, is familiar as the prototype of Father Christmas. In Rumania he symbolises winter and brings good luck [Irimie-Focşa, *Icons on Glass*, 15]. In Russia, where he was greatly beloved, he became patron saint and protector of the land, and several Tsars were named after him. People said: 'If God dies, we still have St Nicholas' [Wallace, 112]. The Grand Duke Vladimir Monomah, a 12th century Russian nobleman, requested an icon of St Nicholas from Kiev and it reached him by swimming across Lake Ilmen [Onasch, 349]. Among the Arctic and Sub-Arctic tribes of Northern Siberia the process of Christian conversion was a slow one and, at the time when the communists expelled all the missionaries, the Tunguz, for example, venerated St Nicholas as protector of the herds and made an offering of reindeer blood and fat smeared on his icon [Kolarz, 86], an interesting cultural transference from earlier practice. Many legends are told of this saint,who is venerated as protector of children, brides and mariners [Wild, 48; Wallace, 112]. All Greek ships used to carry his icon and prayers were said before it for the safety of those on board [Spicer, 154]. He was taken over from the Greeks and Russianised as protector against the Tartars and other invaders [Onasch, 341]. In the monastery of Stavronika on Mount Athos there is a mosaic icon of St Nicholas of the Oyster. An iconoclast is said to have thrown it in the sea,where it remained till it was discovered by fishermen, an oyster growing on its face. Part of the shell is preserved in the monastery and used for ceremonial purposes [Dawkins, 247].

The cult of St Boris and St Gleb, unfamiliar to
us, was widespread in medieval Russia. Sons of
Prince Vladimir of Kiev who were murdered in 1015
after their father's death by their brother
Svyatopolk, they were the first national Russian
saints, warriors who have returned at times of
national crisis to lend aid. They rode with the
men of Novgorod in 1169 against the besieging
armies of Suzdal. In 1380 they accompanied St
Michael and St Demetrius at the head of the Russian armies attacking the Tartars, and in 1240 they
rowed across the River Neva to help Alexander
Nevsky in his battle against the Swedes. They
were seen at night by a watchman, dressed in shining robes and gleaming crowns [Onasch, 380; Howe,
80-]. Nationalism is an important factor here.
The saints have been described as symbols of
princely power, in particular the growing authority of Moscow [Onasch, 380]. There was some opposition to their canonisation, but this disappeared
when their bodies, which were being transferred to
a specially-built church, gave out a sweet-smell-
ing odour [T.Talbot Rice, *Concise History*, 55-6].
In traditional folk belief the devil smells evilly
by contrast with the pleasant savour emanating
from the bodies of the sanctified.

Another warrior saint, St George, is also a
popular figure. There are large numbers of Russian
icons portraying him slaying the dragon, symbol
of evil [Wallace, 120]. Indeed it is one of the
commonest subjects in Orthodox icons [Ouspensky,
141]. He is usually dressed in a red cloak, signi-
fying martyrdom, and rides a white horse emblematic of his purity. The killing of the dragon was
a late medieval addition to the life of the saint,
who is represented as a martyr in the earliest
Greek legends [D.Talbot Rice, 85; Attwater, *Dic.
of Saints*, 148]. David Talbot Rice has suggested
that some earlier popular tale became grafted onto

the life of the Christian saint and martyr [D.Tal-
bot Rice, 85]. An early 7th to 9th century icon at
Mount Sinai shows him mounted and slaying a Bar-
barian,which the dragon represents [Onasch, 356].
He was the Russian patron saint of stables, cattle
and farms,which no doubt he was invoked to protect
against evil beasts [Onasch, 356]. He was also
protector of livestock in Rumania,where he represented the spring [Irimie-Focşa, 15] and where
his icon was often placed in the home. If it continually fell from its hook onto the floor it was an
omen of death for someone in the family. To avoid
this,it was sometimes propped against the wall at
floor level. If it still fell over on its face the
omen was very bad indeed. The icon was then immediately given away to a stranger, over a vessel
filled with water to nullify any possible ill con-
sequences [Information from Professor Vulcănescu].
St George's feast day is April 23rd. Perhaps it is
because of this spring link that the Cypriots
credit him with the power of finding husbands for
young girls. On a Saturday they must knock on the
door of a church dedicated to St George, saying:
'As we knock on the door of your church may a
bridegroom come and knock on our house.' He also
cures the sick and the mentally disturbed at the
new or full moon. A lesser Cypriot festival is
celebrated on November 3rd, before the harvest, in
honour of St George the Farmer [D.Talbot Rice,
161-3].
    An icon of St George 'not made by human hands'
hangs in the Bulgarian monastery of Zográphou on
Mount Athos. There is a smudge on the nose because,
the story goes, a Bishop who looked at the icon
did not believe in its miraculous origin and poked
it to discover the texture of the paint. As a
punishment for doubting,his finger stuck to the
icon and had to be cut off. The smudge is the
remains of his finger. The Bishop of Erissos, the
villain of this story, had attempted to gain con-

trol over the monasteries of Athos and consequently was not popular [Dawkins, 220-1].

St George may contain some elements of the
ancient Slav god Volos, who was protector of herds
and cattle and was especially venerated in Novgorod, where icons of St George were particularly
numerous [Ouspensky, 141; Onasch, 357-8] and where
one of the streets was called Ulica Volosova -
Volos Street. In his warrior aspect we may compare
the invocation in medieval English battle cries:

'The game's afoot,
Follow your spirit; and upon this charge,
Cry, God for Harry, England, and Saint George.'
[*Henry V*.iii.1]

Of course the cross of St George, which was carried
at the Battle of Agincourt (1415), constitutes the
flag of England [Hole, 31-2].

The prophet Elijah is another common subject in
iconography, perhaps because he represents a
Christianisation of the ancient Slav thunder god
Perun, whose attributes as protector against
lightning and fire he seems to have acquired
[Alpatow, 11; De Grunwald, 18] as a result of his
judgment by fire on Mount Carmel and subsequent
translation to heaven in a fiery chariot [Onasch,
378]. Protection against fire was important for a
people like the Russians, who lived in wooden
houses, and Elijah was a popular household icon in
pre-revolutionary times. The farmers especially
venerated him for his supposed control over the
weather, possibly because he mounted into the sky,
where rain originates; the link with Perun is also
pertinent here [Bunt, 98; Wallace, 106]. He occupied a similar position in Rumania [Focşa, 15].

Another icon with an obvious pagan antecedent
is the dog-headed image of St Christopher, one of
the 14 Auxiliary Saints. The first known reference
to the dog-headed saint is in the Gnostic *Acts of
St Bartholomew*, a 4th century Egyptian work. The

apostles St Bartholomew and St Andrew baptise a
cynocephalic man who is terrorising the population
and he accompanies them on missionary work in
Parthia, having given up his horrific ways. In the
reign of Justinian [527-65 A.D.] a dog-headed St
Christopher icon was found in the monastery on
Mount Sinai and the earliest oriental representations showed him thus [Ameisenowa, 42]. It was
not until much later, in the Alpine countries of
the 12th and 13th centuries, that the figure of
the Christ-bearer evolved.

The ancient oriental dog-headed type, which is
of more interest here, was preserved in the Orthodox Church until the 18th century. Only 2 examples
appear to have been recorded in the West: a picture in Usuard's *Martyrology*, a mid 12th century
work in the town library of Stuttgart, and a 16th
century stained-glass window in Angers cathedral,
where the dog-headed figure is combined with the
later concept of the Christ bearer. A 17th century
Russian icon depicting a soldier in profile, with
lance and shield, his dog-head encircled by a
nimbus, suggests a link traceable from Egypt and
the dog-headed god Anubis, through Coptic and
Byzantine tradition to the art of Russia. Christopher was an apotropaic saint: to look at his
image or icon meant one would live till the end of
the day and rest secure from sudden death. His
cult was thus very popular in the Middle Ages and
very widespread. Representations of the dog-headed
figure continue well into the 18th century in
Rumania and Russia, where the cult was opposed by
the Metropolitan of Moscow, Arsenij Macéjević.
Moses Gaster, one of the founders of the Folklore
Society, who was of Rumanian origin, had in his
personal library a Rumanian chapbook printed at
the Monastery of Neamtz by permission of the
Metropolitan of Moldavia. It gives the life of St
Christopher and is illustrated by the dog-headed
image [Ameisenowa, 42-5]. A Western visitor to

Mount Athos in 1935 noted several examples of the figure [Dawkins, 194-5]. The usual explanation is that the saint's handsome face led him into grave temptation with women, so he prayed to be given this dog's head in its place [Dawkins, 195]. Understandably, many examples of the cult must have been lost through the activities of the iconoclasts.

Icons help the Orthodox to regard the saints not as remote but as protectors and friends [Ware, 261]. Some are associated with particular trades and professions. Saints Florus and Laurus, who probably never existed, and were said to have been drowned in a well by the order of the Emperor Licinius, were the patron saints of grooms and horses [Attwater, *Dic. of Saints*, 132; Talbot Rice, *Russian Art*, 70]. Many were beloved for their protective intercessionary powers. In Rumania the icon of St Haralambios offers protection against the plague and other diseases, which he tramples underfoot in the form of an ugly skeleton or dragon. Icons of this saint are used to cure disease by direct application, because he is closely linked with the terrible epidemics of cholera and leprosy that decimated south-eastern Europe in the 18th and 19th centuries. Such icons, painted on sheepskin, fabric or bark, were ceremonially stuck on the diseased part of the body and left in position until they came off, when they were burnt and consumed as an antidote. Rumanian icons of this type were also used to cure malaria, St Anthony's fire, and epilepsy [Information from Professor Vulcănescu].

In the same country St John is invoked to safeguard the livestock [Irimie and Focşa, 15]. In Cyprus the icon of St John assists children slow in learning to talk. Their parents hang a wax tongue as a votive offering before his icon, light the lamp, and smear a little of the oil on the child's tongue [Talbot Rice, 165].

The Cypriot saints form a group of their own,

for many of them are peculiar to Cyprus and the usual Orthodox Saints acquired specific legends of miraculous powers. Praying before the icons was a cure for every malady known to man: St Marina alleviates insomnia, St Nicholas removes warts, and St Vichinos looks after coughs and colds. This last saint was an ascetic who went naked, dressed only in his long hair. Perhaps this is why there are so few icons of him in existence. Those who made offerings to him brought thread draped round their necks and this was used for making candlewicks [Talbot Rice, 159, 167, 169].

St Mamas, a famous Cypriot hermit who lived in a cave near Morphou, was arrested for tax evasion by the Byzantine Duke of his day: taxes went towards the upkeep of roads and other amenities which the saint never used. The soldiers escorting him to Nicosia for trial were startled by a lion, not a usual Cypriot animal, which sprang out in front of the Saint and made as if to gobble up a small woolly lamb. The Saint at once picked up the lamb, mounted the lion and rode it to Nicosia into the Duke's throneroom, a symbolism recalling the famous passage from *Isaiah*. The surprised ruler exempted St Mamas from taxes for the rest of his life. The hermit then devoted himself to milking lions and using their cheese to feed the poor [Talbot Rice, 166]. The Turks chased him so that some of the milk was split and they say the place can still be seen in the village of Alays, Turkey. Leontios Makhairas wrote in his Chronicle: 'And wherever they set up his picture there is an abundance of cures...if I were to write the cures he worked, I should not make an end as long as I live' [Makhairas, 33]. Cures of this kind could be quite spectacular. In 1769 a boy named John, of Nicosia, was troubled with bouts of insanity. His parents took him before the icon of St Heraclides on the feast day of the saint. The boy at once vomited a snake a span long and two crabs, and was

pronounced cured. The reptiles are hanging up in
the church as a witness to the miracle [Talbot
Rice, 164].

In Russian tradition several saints are domin-
ated by their symbolic role, so that they are more
in the nature of abstractions. Thus St Anastasia
represents the Resurrection and St Paraskeva or
Pjanitza is the personification of Good Friday;
Pjanitza is Russian for Friday, the fifth (*Pjatyi*)
day of the week [Hamilton, 67].

This tendency towards abstraction is the exception rather than the rule. Generally speaking
icons assume many of the attributes of human
beings. The iconoclasts seem to have feared their
large staring eyes [cf. Dawkins, 314]. In Serbia
the Moslems pierced what they thought were Evil
Eyes [Stewart, 76], and here we may compare the
action of Patriarch Nikon [1655], who put out the
eyes of offending western-influenced icons and
paraded them through the streets of Moscow. Dournovo refers to an Armenian Gospel of 1323, decorated
with a picture of an angel putting out the devil's
eyes [Dournovo, 148-9]. Cecil Stewart, discussing
Serbian religious paintings, makes an interesting
point when he suggests that artistically they
establish a direct link with the observer; evil
beings tend to be shown in profile, so that they
cannot receive the direct gaze of the worshipper
[Stewart, 45]. For it is the Orthodox belief that
holy figures appear in icons and can therefore be
prayed to [French, 133]. It has even been suggested that the face of Abraham was cut out of the
10th century Etchmedzian Gospels, so that it should
not come in contact with the face of the Virgin on
the opposite page when the book was closed [Dourn-
ovo, 26-7].

In Rumania a cycle of legends relates to wander-
ing icons which travel at night, usually from an
impure to a pure place, or from a sacred site to
one requiring consecration. Many chapels or road-

93

side crosses with icons are said to have been
founded on the basis of this belief [Information
from Professor Vulcănescu]. The icon of Soumela
monastery, some distance from Trebizond, flew
through the air guided by 2 angels and came to
rest shining brightly [Dawkins, 159]. These foundation legends are a commonplace in iconography.

There are stories of icons that bleed: Arabs in
conquered cities are said to have become exceed-
ingly ill from the blood which flowed from damaged
icons [Gerhard, 26]. They also speak, weep, fall,
move, swim, strike down wrong-doers, protect their
own, and undertake supernatural journeys, not only
to indicate the site for a new church or monastery,
but also to escape the depredations of the pagans.

We may say then that the functions of the icon
are highly varied: they are protective, curative,
rain-inducing, explanatory, redressing wrongs,
administering punishment, providing supernatural
sanctioning of paths for the individual and
political action for the state, underscoring
decisions taken by strengthening hope and courage,
and providing a focal point for nationalistic
feeling and endeavour. They supply a safeguard
against the elements and an explanation for
puzzling events. They enforce the status quo in
various ways like conversion of the heathen and
the relative position of the sexes. A cycle of
legends from Mount Athos describes royal consorts
who attempted to break the ban on women entering
the churches. A voice issues from the icon of the
Virgin saying: 'Go no further: in this place there
is another Queen than thou' [Dawkins, 102, 113]. A
version of the Portaitissa legend explains that
this is why the famous icon was placed on the gate
instead of in the church. That an icon of the
Virgin should feature in a prohibition against
women is an interesting psychological factor.

Reprimands administered by an icon varied in
severity. A picture of the Virgin admonished a

94

group of Bulgarian monks from Mount Athos, who
carried it to the seashore for their Easter ceremonies and became drunk following an over-indulg-
ent picnic. The icon, as a sign of disapproval,
became very heavy and could not be lifted [Dawkins,
251]. This happened in the 14th century. An unpleasant surprise lay in store for a lazy sacris-
tan, also on Mount Athos, who neglected to light
the lamp in front of the Kosinitsa Virgin. One day
he was standing near it, when a hand shot out of
the icon and struck him a violent blow. This
legend appears to be an attempt to explain the
absence of the silver covering on the right hand
of the icon [Dawkins, 366].

Tamara Talbot Rice notes that it is often icons
of outstanding quality and beauty which were
credited with possession of miraculous powers
[Talbot Rice, *Russian Icons*, 10-11]. Another
authority of Russian origin has pointed out that
more than 200 wonder-working icons existed in pre-
Soviet times [Iswolsky, 147] according to extant
Russian ecclesiastical records. Much of the
material relating to these wonder-working icons
belongs to the area of folk religion rather than
formal religion [French, 133]. This becomes increasingly apparent when we consider that in
Rumania paint was scraped from the icons from, for
example, the eyes, nose, or mouth, to cure analogous parts of the body that were diseased; the
paint was used as an ingredient in traditional
medicines [Information from Professor Vulcănescu].
The curative powers of paint and plaster from
church paintings were also treasured in Serbia,
where they were mixed with oil to produce a popular ointment [Stewart, 76]. We find analogous
practices in our own country, for example in
Devonshire, where gratings from statues in Exeter
Cathedral were utilised for medicinal purposes
[Brown, *Folklore*. LXXII.392].

The curative power of oil from an icon lamp has

already been noted in relation to Cyprus. In 1915
a Russian gave an icon to a monastery on Mount
Athos as a thank-offering for the lamp oil, which
he rubbed on his scalp to cure his baldness. It
has also been swallowed as a remedy for toothache
[Dawkins, 182, 344]. In 1958 an Anglican monk
visiting the shrine of St Sergius at Zagorsk was
told by an elderly woman that oil from the lamps
in front of the icons possessed curative powers.
She added that it was, however, necessary to believe
in the efficacy of the prayers of the blessed
Father Sergius [Tweedy, 14]. St Sergius [c.1314-
1392], founder of Holy Trinity Monastery, was the
first Russian saint to have had mystical experiences, and when he blessed a follower unearthly
light flickered at his finger tips [Wallace, 98].

Evidently the cult of St Sergius continues,
even if under difficulties, in atheist Soviet
Russia, but the icon as a focus of religious power
is recognised and disliked by the regime. They
have been described in a volume by a Communist
author as cult objects with an important role to
play [Nicolescu, 13-14]. The following quote from
Ogónek, an official party publication, sets out
the Soviet attitude: 'Every day many people enter
our country. But among the many open-hearted
people one still encounters individuals with
hidden luggage compartments. These respectable
looking gentlemen, giddy atomic blondes, or sweet-
looking older ladies, smuggle in goods in suit-
cases with false bottoms. Sometimes narcotics,
sometimes banknotes, but some bring in religious
literature, all kinds of crosses and icons. How
much harm this can do! How many people can be made
unhappy! How many lives crippled!' [Ogónek, Moscow,
Nov. 1963, 30-31. Quoted by Mandel, 37-8]. Various
points are of interest here: not only the attempt
to discredit missionary activities by lumping them
together with drug pedlars and currency swindlers,
but also the striking negative reference to the

96

icon as a symbol of power. The full significance
of the icon as a focus of religious belief, and in
its semi-human aspect, was clearly recognised by
the Soviet authorities, as the following report
from *Pravda* illustrates. It is dated Christmas
1922, the early period following the Soviet seiz-
ure of government, when the Komsomols were in the
habit of organising so-called 'carnivals' at
Christmas time. Here is a description of one at
Rostov: 'The Komsomols burned Jehovah, Allah,
Christ, and the Mother of God — They burned as
though they were alive, they shrivelled, their
heads drooped, and their hands shook' [Zatko, 118]
Here the folk tradition of the icon as capable of
human behaviour has been taken up and amplified,
presumably with the intention of lessening the
effectiveness of the power symbol.

Tradition is a potent force in human society
and any new system of thought is wise to take
cognisance of what has gone before and adapt
accordingly. Thus one sees many religious symbols
and motifs reappear in Communist mythology in
changed and altered form. The Dove, emblem of the
Holy Spirit in numerous icons, has become the
universal symbol of Communist brotherhood. The
fine, levied before the Revolution for accidently
killing a symbol of the Holy Spirit, is still
theoretically levied for accidently killing the
symbol of Communist brotherhood [Personal observation, Moscow 1962]. Similarly St Nicholas and his
associations with Christmas have been transformed
into the secular New Year celebrations centred
around the folk figure of Grandfather Frost. There
are also traces of the cult of the Virgin in the
mother theme of Soviet art [Billington, 200]. I
have myself had an opportunity to meet a Soviet
revolutionary mother, a concept underlined and encouraged in an attempt to raise the birthrate.
Those who have borne more than a certain quota of
children receive a medal from the Kremlin and are

97

greatly honoured. The cult of the Virgin, as I
pointed out earlier, laid emphasis not on Virginity but on Motherhood.

The transitional stage is of particular
interest. Fletcher refers to a church which put up
portraits of Lenin and Kalinin next to the icons
[Fletcher, 64-5]. This was at the end of the 1920s.
During the period after the Nazi-Soviet pact of
1939-41 had been broken by Hitler's invasion, but
the honeymoon between the Russian people and the
German people was still in force, Engelhardt found
the parish priest of Klinzy, in South West Russia,
displaying a picture of Hitler beside the icons in
the Holy Corner of his house [Engelhardt, 117]. In
Soviet Russia the modern icon is an enormous
portrait poster — one sees them everywhere, in the
streets, main squares, factories, public buildings,
and on parade — portraits of the founders of
Communism: Lenin, Marx, Engels, and the party
leaders. The skill of the icon painter lives on in
the beautiful boxes decorated with traditional
scenes and executed by the artists of Palekh, a
former icon village [Talbot Rice, *Russian Icons*,
20; Gerhard, 204].

Information on religious practice is difficult
to obtain from Soviet Russia; but there is evidence, not only that it continues [cf. the various
books and articles by Michael Bourdeaux], but that
icons are treasured even by products of the
present system. In 1973 the journalist Michael
Frayn visited the flat of a designer in Moscow:
'Another wall was lined with built-in bookcases,
and all the rest with icons — row upon row of sad-
eyed saints and Mothers of God, watching a skating
competition on television. I saw a lot of icons
in the apartments I visited...Surrounded by his
icons, the host puts on Soviet recordings of Tom
Jones and Engelbert Humperdinck, and fixes drinks'
[*Observer*, March 4, 1973]. The strange power of the
icon lives on even under atheism. I was amused to

be told recently, by a colleague from a Communist country with a neurotic wife, that every time he returns home from a field trip, she takes him before the icons and makes him swear that he has not been unfaithful with the village girls.

Acknowledgments

I am most grateful to Wendy Boase for very considerable assistance in the preparation of this paper. I am also much indebted to the following for advice, help and information: Cornelia Belcin, Father Richard Hayes, Father Herbert Moore, John Norman, Valerie Vrioni and Professor Romulus Vulcănescu.

5. QUEST FOR THE GREEN MAN

K.H.Basford

THE FOLIATE HEAD is one of the strangest of all
the strange and fanciful motifs of decorative
sculpture seen in the medieval churches of western
Europe and, since it occurs so often, is probably
the most familiar. Its decorative possibilities
are, perhaps, sufficient to explain its popularity.
It could be manipulated to suit any position where
ornament was required and was frequently used on
roof bosses, capitals, corbels, tympana, screens,
misericords, arm rests, bench ends and poppy heads,
also on fonts and tombs. But it was not repeated
merely as a useful 'stock figure' and it is rare
to find two that are exactly alike. The idea of a
face in the leaves could excite an imaginative
response and the individual craftsman could im-
provise on the theme and create his own fantastic
variation of the motif.

Many of these carvings are sinister. Some of
them are powerful fantasies of the eerie and
macabre. There are but few benevolent, smiling
faces; occasionally they smile, but equivocally,
like mischievous, even malicious imps. The expressions are, more typically, sad or grim. The
forehead is contracted in a frown and the eyes
glare. Sometimes the eyes are squinting, suggest-
ing various levels of inebriation, bellicose,
morose, even comatose but seldom jocose. Sometimes
the faces are partially or almost wholly hidden
behind the leaves, secret faces, peering through
gaps in the foliage.

It was the discovery of such faces under the
leaves, carved on roof bosses in the Lady Chapel
of Ely Cathedral, that first suggested a resemblance to the Green Man, or Jack in the Green,
peeping through the leaves with which he was
covered when he played his part in the ceremonies

on May Day.[1] The foliate head was, however, more positively identified as the Green Man by Lady Raglan, and explained in this way in an article in *Folklore* in 1939,[2] since which time the figure, in all its variant forms, has been popularly called the Green Man.

Although the Green Man explanation cannot be stretched to fit and cover every example of the motif as it was used in the Middle Ages, the image does, in fact, display at least one Green Man characteristic, namely, his power of revival and regeneration. It is, perhaps, because of its remarkable and enduring vitality that it can be of interest to folklore studies. It provides an illustration of how an inherited, or traditional theme can evolve and diversify as it is exposed to different cultural climates and as it interests and catches the imagination of the particular individuals who use it. In his essay, Continuity and Variation in the Meaning of Images, Fritz Saxl pointed out that 'images with a meaning peculiar to their own time and place, once created, have a magnetic power to attract other ideas into their sphere...'[3] The author believed that visual images no less than written documents could give valuable insights into the thoughts, ideas and even dreams of the people who made them, and undoubtedly the foliate head attracted many ideas into its sphere during the course of its long history. Each example can be studied as a historical document, reflecting some of the ideas which shaped it at a particular time and in a particular place, and also as a personal document, left to us by an individual craftsman who, though he may sometimes have been an illiterate man, unable to put his thoughts and feelings into writing, could express the strangest and most subtle ideas and fantasies in his carvings.

My personal quest for the Green Man began with a memorable encounter with the foliate head on the

Tomb of Saint-Abre, 4th or 5th century, at Saint Hilaire-le-Grand, Poitiers

Cast of 'Green Man' capital, Trier cathedral
Rheinisches Landesmuseum, Trier

Green Man keystone at Fountains Abbey, dated 1483

walls of Fountains Abbey, as I mentioned in a
letter to *Folklore* in 1968.[4] The sad face of this
withered old man seemed to me the most human touch
left in the ruins and yet, at the same time, the
most ghostly. It is a macabre image and certainly
could not be interpreted as a Jack in the Green.
Not only would a Jack in the Green make nonsense
in this austere Cistertian building, but the der-
elict head, invaded and overtaken by a weird
growth of vegetation, is an image of death and
ruin rather than of life and resurrection. The
foliate head at Fountains is a very personal document but before I could understand it I had to
learn how to read it as a historical document.

The foliate head, or leaf mask, originated in
Roman art during the second half of the first century, A.D.,[5] but it is generally considered rather
as a second century motif since this was the
period of its formal development. It was sometimes
used as a repeated motif in the 'peopled scroll'
ornament, and sometimes as an isolated motif. A
series of male masks with acanthus sprouting from
their faces were used to decorate friezes on both
the triumphal arches of Septimus Severus in Rome
and on Aurelian's Temple of the Sun, also in
Rome,[6] but the motif was widespread throughout the
eastern and western parts of the Empire. It was
used on temples serving many different deities and
also on sarcophagi, in much the same way as the
medusa mask. It has, in fact, been described as a
male medusa,[7] and one example, carved on the fa-
çade of a temple at Hatra in Mesopotamia (the
modern Al Hadr, Iraq) and now believed to date
from the mid-second century, has snakes winding
in his hair. His face has leaves, either acanthus
or sea weed, growing on the cheeks and chin in
place of the normal hairy whiskers and beard. But
the most striking feature of the Hatra mask is its
intense, glowering expression. It bears a remarkable resemblance to the scowling male medusa on

the Roman pediment at Bath[8] though this is not a
leaf mask. The Bath medusa has also been compared
with the frowning Okeanos mask on the central
medallion of the great silver dish from Mildenhall
(now in the British Museum).[9] The Mildenhall
Okeanos has a beard of sea weed or acanthus and
dolphins swimming through his wild, wavy locks.
The penetrating, baleful glare, common to all
three masks, is a persistent though not invariable
characteristic of the antique leaf masks. It must
be recognised as a 'family trait', and it was inherited by many of the medieval Green Men.

Other, quite different prototypes of the Green
Man are found on fragments from the funerary monuments discovered at Neumagen, on the Mosel, not
far from Trier.[10] These monuments, which date from
the second and third centuries, were made to com-
memorate wealthy Treveran citizens, many of whom
were wine merchants, and some are actually in the
form of wine ships, manned by a crew of sailors —
some of them very merry. The leaf masks which
appear on several of these magnificent memorials
have been cited as being among the most important
for the development of the motif in countries
north of the Alps.[11] One of them almost certainly
represents Okeanos who, in this context, would
symbolise a safe and prosperous voyage to the
Islands of the Blessed. The meaning of the others
is not so clear. The leaf mask which is the central feature of a large sculpture panel from the
Iphigenienpfeiler has, on one side of it, a cymbal
with a shepherd's crook stuck through it[12] and
these objects may have Bacchic significance since
maenads clashed cymbals and satyrs carried crooked
sticks.[13] Bacchic themes were, of course, often
used on pagan tombs and symbolised the happy after-
life. It is tempting to wonder whether the leaf
mask also refers to some aspect of the Bacchic
cult. In the ancient revels held in honour of
Dionysos the participants stained their faces with

new wine and put on great beards made out of leaves.[14] On the other hand, Okeanos is often used side by side with Bacchic themes as, for example, on the Mildenhall dish, so this leaf mask might well represent Okeanos.

The Neumagen leaf masks are very variable in form and range from the type in which the leafy element is subordinate to the human element — reduced to a mere frill of acanthus beard and whisker on the fleshy chin and cheeks and a curly acanthus eyebrow, to the type where the human face is completely veiled by acanthus (as on the *Iphigenienpfeiler*) with the leaves not only substituting for the facial hair but growing from the tear glands in the corners of the eyes and from the inside of the mouth, and, finally, to the type which is all leaves — the human element suggested by the folding and overlapping of the deeply lobed acanthus. Two faces representative of this extreme type are discovered in a frieze from the *Schulreliefpfeiler*. The frieze is filled with sensitively carved acanthus and the faces are formed, it would seem, as though by a chance arrangement of the leaves. Yet they are so skilfully portrayed that although nothing remains of human flesh they are full of human feeling. How can a cluster of leaves seem so grief stricken? Perhaps because, in this complete metamorphosis, it is suggested that the sad faces are no more than a memory.

The Neumagen monuments are now in the Rheinisches Landesmuseum in Trier, and here also are two casts taken from the superb leaf masks which were introduced into Trier Cathedral in the sixth century. The casts are the only visible evidence we have today of these leaf masks, since the originals are walled up in the Cathedral behind masonry erected during the course of restoration in the eleventh century. They were discovered about a hundred years ago when excavations were carried out at the time of a further restoration.

The temporary removal of part of the eleventh
century masonry gave access to one of the four
pillars set up in the Square Chancel by Bishop
Nicetius in the sixth century. The lavishly carved
composite capital had, for its principal ornament,
a huge leaf mask on each face, between the volutes.
The cast, taken at the time of this brief exposure,
shows a leaf crowned head with more leaves spread-
ing over the brow and growing on the cheeks, from
under the eyes and from the sides of the nose. The
upper lip has been broken and because of this
damage the expression of the face is somewhat
distorted, but the great eyes, rolling up under
the leafy brows, show that it was a deeply serious
expression. Traces of pigment found on the capital
indicated that it had been painted in bright
colours, the leaf masks and volutes golden yellow
and the acanthus ornament below them red.

At the time of the nineteenth century excavations[15] it was generally, but not unanimously
agreed that the capitals were contemporary with
the sixth century pillars and had been carved by
Italian craftsmen working from Byzantine models.
Their true date, the second century, was not finally established until the excavations of 1961 to
1963,[16] when the original material was subjected
to a more rigorous scrutiny and studied in con-
junction with researches concurrently undertaken
on the site of the temple Am Herrenbrünnchen.[17]
It is now accepted that the capitals had originally belonged to this Hadrianic temple and that
Bishop Nicetius had recovered them from the ruins
and used them, at second hand, for his new pillars
in the Cathedral. We must assume that Bishop
Nicetius had admired the excellent workmanship and
splendid appearance of these figured capitals and
had chosen them for these qualities and not for
their subject matter. The foliate head came into
the Cathedral, as it were, by accident. But it was
an event of great importance for the motif and

106

probably marked a turning point in its history.

The beautiful leaf mask capitals were displayed in Trier Cathedral for five hundred years. They were, no doubt, a conspicuous ornament in the Square Chancel, an area of special sanctity, planned round a curious architectural feature which was very likely the repository of some precious relic, perhaps a fragment of the True Cross, or the Seamless Robe, now preserved in the Cathedral Treasury.[18] In Trier, the leaf mask began its new life in the service of the church in particularly auspicious and favourable circumstances. Sanctioned by long use in this venerable church, in one of the earliest and most important strongholds of Christianity in the west, it could pass easily into medieval art.

Although it must be recognised that it was probably this chance introduction into the Cathedral in Trier that gave the foliate head a secure place in the church, we cannot be sure that, but for this happy accident, it would not have survived. Even before Bishop Nicetius had 'adopted' it, the motif had found a small niche in Christian ornament. A foliate head is carved in shallow relief on the base of the marble lid of the tomb of Saint Abre in the Church of Saint-Hilaire-le-Grand in Poitiers.[19] This Christian tomb, which dates from the fourth or fifth century, is decorated with motifs borrowed from pagan tombs. They include dolphins, a rayed bust, and a vase containing foliage as well as the foliate head. It is a curious carving, quite unlike the Hellenistic leaf masks. The head is surrounded by contiguous and overlapping leaves which may represent the hair and beard, while large sprays of stylised foliage and flowers spring from the nostrils and extend on either side of the head, like fantastic moustaches. This modest work is of great interest, not only because it is such an early example in Christian ornament, but because of its originality.

It does not so much look backward to the Hellenistic leaf masks from which it undoubtedly derives
as forward, perhaps providing a prototype for the
early medieval figures with sprays of foliage
coming out of the nose.

There are no foliate heads, nor other fantastic
creatures, in the eastern church. This is possibly
explained by the fact that from the eighth century
there was strong opposition to the use of imagery.
The absence of the foliate head certainly cannot
be explained by any lack of inspiring models.
There is much evidence to show that the leaf mask
was a popular architectural ornament in Constantinople and in other places around the Bosphoros
and the Sea of Marmora in the sixth century.
Beautiful examples in the Hellenistic tradition
were still being produced in this region at the
very time that the motif was beginning its new
lease of life in the western church. Several
figured capitals, all of them dating from the
sixth century, with leaf masks as their only or
dominant motif, have been collected by the Archaeological Museum in Istanbul and included among
them are some very recent discoveries, still un-
published at the time of my visit in 1973. All
these leaf masks go by the name of Okeanos, although it is recognised that some are more complex
characters and do not refer exclusively to the old
sea god.

On the extremely elegant capital, discovered at
Mudanya on the southern shores of the Sea of Marmora in 1885, are two leaf masks of great nobility.
They are placed at the angles on one side of the
capital and are separated by a horn of plenty
which has an acanthus leaf at the base and grapes
brimming over the lip, and, suspended above it, a
leaf from the plane tree with a ripe pod on the
left of it and an ear of wheat on the right. The
masks, which are exactly matched, have been described as figures of Okeanos under a type which

108

is at once satyr and sea god.[20] The hair, eyebrows, whiskers, moustache and beard are formed
from finely dissected acanthus. The faces have
both strength and delicacy and an expression of
sombre gravity. The forehead is slightly furrowed
and the eyes, with their deeply incised pupils,
stare out into space, preoccupied with inner
vision. The carving is exquisitely refined. The
leaves, especially those which sweep back from the
eyebrows and spread over the temples, look fresh,
turgid and resilient. Every detail is cleanly and
crisply defined, but all this detail is poised in
the marvellous balance, harmony and unity of the
whole design. Attention must be drawn to one
detail, perhaps not of any great significance in
itself, but interesting because it is found again,
as an 'inherited character', in many medieval leaf
heads. This is the transverse ridge of flesh, just
above the bridge of the nose.

A second capital, of unknown provenance, has
leaf masks of the satyr type on each of its four
faces. Two large acanthus leaves, growing from
either side of a narrow vertical fold of flesh,
just above the nose, rise up like branching horns,
or antlers. Two more large leaves grow from the
sides and base of the nose, to form the moustache,
while a fifth leaf, growing from under the full
lower lip, hangs down over the chin to form the
beard. The face is clearly indicated as a mask,
cut off in a straight line across the forehead,
and yet the mask-like appearance is contradicted
by the intensity of the expression. The curiously
elongated eyes, with their barely focused pupils,
have a look of rapt introspection. The mysterious
intensity of expression, with the gaze concentrated on the inner rather than the outer world,
is characteristic of all the masks on these two
capitals. It is to be seen again in innumerable
Green Man carvings as an alternative to the baleful, or hostile glare which is directed outwards.

Two leaf masks, one on each of a pair of capitals
discovered in Istanbul on the site now occupied by
the New Palace of Justice, are represented with
the pupils of the eyes converging in a quite
definite squint. This exaggeration of the 'barely
focused look' produces, of course, a quite different expression. Was it a deliberate modification?

The horn of plenty appears again side by side
with leaf masks on a capital discovered in the old
City Wall in 1972. This second example may indicate that the juxtaposition of the two motifs was
more than mere coincidence. One more capital must
be mentioned. It was very recently discovered at
Kanlica on the Bosphoros and shows a rather fleshy
featured Okeanos with an elaborate coiffure of
stylised foliage which branches out on either side
of the head in 'ram's horn' spirals. Leaves grow
out of the folds of the cheeks and at each side of
the full-lipped mouth. The eyes are large and
staring and the eyebrows. which in this case are
not represented as leafv, are strongly contracted
towards the nose and move obliquely towards the
temples. He is a glowering, profoundly perplexed
creature, both inwardly disturbed and outwardly
hostile.

It is at the risk of tedium I have recorded so
much detail, but it is only on the basis of such
detailed observation that the 'iconography' can be
established. It is, I believe, necessary to recognise and, indeed, to memorise, the particulars
of the antique leaf masks, even though their
significance cannot always be understood or evalu-
ated, so that these various threads of tradition
can be followed as they are picked up again, sometimes after centuries of neglect, and woven into
new patterns in the Middle Ages. Among the multi-
tude of foliated figures in the manuscripts and
carvings produced in the tenth, eleventh and
twelfth centuries there are few which bear any
close resemblance to the Okeanos masks of late

antiquity (sometimes only the frown and the glare remain, like the Cheshire Cat in reverse), neither can they be readily recognised as Green Men. The elements of the former are dissolved in a world of fluid fantasy, and it is not until the beginning of the thirteenth century that the Green Man emerges from the melting pot.

I suspect that the fire that heated the pot into which Okeanos was thrown was hell-fire. The leaf mask became demonic. This change of direction is clearly illustrated in two manuscripts produced at Reichenau or Trier. The first of these, a Psalter, was presented to Egbert, Archbishop of Trier, in 983. The dedicatory miniature is framed by a border of human masks linked together by acanthus scroll. Although the faces are rather goblin-like and the foliage sprouts from the mouth and not from the cheeks the idea is obviously derived from the leaf masks in the Hellenistic 'peopled scroll' motif. In the border of the corresponding dedication page of the *Codex Egberti*, presented to Egbert two years later, the human masks are replaced by horrific hollow demon masks with snakes crawling out of their ears. The thoughts that lie behind this extraordinary change can be traced to Rabanus Maurus, an erudite and influential eighth century theologian who was Abbot of Fulda and Archbishop of Mainz. In the *Patrologia Latina*, 112 col. 1037[21] we read: '*Ramus voluptas carnis, ut in Ezechiele: "Ecce applicant ramum ad nares suos", quod reprobi in voluntate carnis delectantur...Per ramos homines pravi, ut in Job: "Ramos ejus arefaciet flamma, quod homines pravos vastabit damnatio aeterna".*' According to him, the leaves represented the sins of the flesh, lustful and wicked men doomed to eternal damnation. Early medieval leaf imagery often reflects such thoughts. Men are seen hopelessly entangled in coiling branches, tormented by evil creatures of the demon wood. We have a splendid example of this

in the Job miniature in the twelfth century
Winchester Bible, (MS. Auct.E. Infra 1.f.304) in
the Bodleian Library, Oxford.

The evil aspect of the leaf mask is nowhere
more strikingly represented than in the remarkable
imagery carved in relief on the facade of San
Pietro, at Toscanella. It is, basically, a 'peopled
scroll' ornament, framing an open, colonnaded
window. The leafy scrolls issue from two monstrous
masks, centrally placed in the upper and lower
borders of the frame. Both masks are in the form
of a tricephalos, a head with three faces, one
presented in frontal view, the other two in profile. Each face has its own mouth and nose but
shares with the others a single pair of eyes. In
medieval imagery the tricephalos could symbolise
either the Holy Trinity or Absolute Evil.[22] The
two directly opposite iconological applications do
not, of course, derive from one another, but each
derives independently from a Gallo-Roman prototype
(extremely common in the region of Reims). There
can be no doubt which of these two meanings is intended here, at Toscanella. The two monsters are
similar but not identical. In both cases the
centre face sticks his tongue out while the faces
in profile stick out, not a fleshy tongue, but a
long 'tongue' of foliated scroll. Each three-faced
demon has, however, his own diabolical attributes.
The upper one is horned and the lower one, which
is attached to a torso, clasps a writhing serpent
to his bosom and the snake, like his master,
sticks out his venomous tongue. Though we must
recognise that these extraordinary images are
based on the old leaf mask, there are a number of
added features, the demon horns and the sticking
out tongue and the tricephalic form. This twelfth
century carving illustrates very clearly the point
made by Saxl, that images can behave like magnets
and attract many different ideas into their sphere.

Once an attribute has been picked up it tends

112

to recur intermittently. Tricephalic Green Men
are rare, but examples are found in fifteenth century misericord carvings in Whalley Church and
Cartmel Priory, both in north Lancashire. A horned
Green Man occupies the corner of a thirteenth century lintel on the portal of Saint-Urbain in Troyes,
while Green Men with the tongue sticking out are
too numerous to mention, though particularly
bizarre examples can be seen in Ely Cathedral and
in St.Teilo's, Llantilio Crossenny, Monmouthshire,
respectively. This last mentioned example also has
leaves growing out of the nose, but before pro-
ceeding to discuss this feature reference must be
made to another idea picked up in the early Middle
Ages. This is the cat face. Other foliated beasts
occur from time to time, but the cat mask is by
far the most common. Foliated cat masks frequently
appear in manuscripts, mainly as a motif in the
elaborately decorated initials, particularly in
the Beatus initial of the Psalter where it is used
to form the bar between the two bows of the letter
B. Cat-face is also found in carvings and an
interesting example appears on a capital in St.
Kyneburga's, at Castor, near Peterborough. This,
apparently, is an anthropomorphic feline since it
grasps the branches growing out of the mouth with
human hands.

Also at Castor are examples of the human or
demon mask with foliated branches coming out of
the nostrils. This type, very common in twelfth
century carvings, has been described as a 'leaf-
demon', perhaps to be interpreted according to the
text quoted by Rabanus Maurus, 'See, how they hold
branches to the nose' Ezekiel, 8.17.[23] Even
though we cannot be certain of the precise meaning
we can have little doubt that this and other types
of foliated figure used in early medieval art
allude to the 'damned in the demon-wood'. The idea
of branches growing out of the nose probably
originates as a modification of the foliate

moustache and the earliest example I have recorded, on St.Abre's tomb in Poitiers, does not appear to represent a demon. But from the tenth century to the end of the twelfth, the leaf mask in all its weird and mutant forms seems to belong, rather exclusively, to the realm of demonography, and the demon nature persists, to some extent at least, in the Green Man.

The changes in architectural style that took place in the early thirteenth century, first in France but soon afterwards in Germany and, rather later, in England, required a corresponding change in the style of ornament, and it was probably the new interest in leaf ornament that opened the way for the appearance of the Green Man. Before discussing this development, however, mention must be made of a foliate head which, though it clearly belongs to the Green Man story, represents an exceptional, possibly unique episode in it. It is carved on the rim of the basin of a fountain made in or about the year 1200 for the Cloisters of Saint-Denis, and is one of a series of heads, each one representing a different Roman deity. Every head has the name of the god inscribed above it, and the name given to the leaf mask is Silvan.[24] This Silvanus is an iconographical puzzle, since Silvanus was never represented in the form of a leaf mask in antiquity and there is no evidence to suggest that the foliate head was widely known as Silvanus in the Middle Ages.[25] It has oak leaves growing from the brow and is rather similar to the Bacchus figure illustrated in the Encyclopedia of Rabanus Maurus.[26] It would seem, therefore, that the artist had simply imagined the woodland god in this form, and used the motif to express his own idea.

The foliate heads of the thirteenth century fall into two main types, the *Tête de Feuilles* and the *Masque Feuillu* (respectively named *Blattmaske* and *Maske im Ranken* in Germany). Both forms are

114

extremely variable. Several examples of the *Tête de Feuilles* are illustrated in the sketch book of the master mason, Villard de Honnecourt.[27] The *Tête de Feuilles* differs from the *Masque Feuillu* in that in the former the human and leafy elements are fused together into one 'organic' whole, whereas in the latter the two elements are distinct and separate entities no matter how intimately they are interwoven. The *Tête de Feuilles* is, therefore, more closely related to the antique leaf masks, while the *Masque Feuillu* is more obviously developed from the 'leaf-demons' with branches growing from the mouth, nose or ears. The two types cannot, however, be regarded as two distinct motifs because intermediate forms can be found, partly of one type, partly of the other.

The most important change that came over the foliate head in the thirteenth century was the change in the leaves. Often they seem to have been observed directly from nature. This was an extraordinary innovation, since a love of nature was at variance with the teaching of the Church which tended to regard all plant and brute nature as belonging to the Devil. Native plants such as oak, ivy, vine, hops, hawthorn, bryony, buttercups, maple and mugwort are suddenly recognised with pleasure, and the carvings often reflect objective curiosity and sheer sensuous enjoyment. Sometimes the interest is focused almost wholly on the leaves and the mask is treated somewhat perfunctorily. Such is the case at Southwell. Several foliate heads appear in the Chapter House, but the human heads are indifferently treated while the leaves, in marked contrast, are portrayed with marvellous sensitivity and almost quiver with life.[28] So obvious is the delight in leaves at Southwell that we might think nature had been reprieved, but this could be a false impression, an oversimplification of the situation. It may be that the leaves, once they were acknowledged to be beautiful, were made to show forth the glory of God even though, by nature, they belonged to the Devil.

It is, perhaps the foliate head that helps to keep us on the right track. The motif, as it now develops as the Green Man, permits a deeper exploration of the ambivalent relationship between man and nature. It is, of course, an intuitive exploration, not in any way scientific. The thinking and feeling are grounded in Christian teaching. The leafy element, represented not only by acanthus but also by foliage deriving from plants growing in northern countries, becomes more luxuriant and the head from which such prolific vegetation springs can seem the very personification of springtime and 'summer is i-comen in'. But the imagery is ambiguous. The face in the leaves can send shivers up the spine. The Green Man can be beautiful and sinister simultaneously. This indeed is what makes him so fascinating. The most beautiful foliate head of the thirteenth century, and perhaps of all time, is the acanthus mask under the Rider statue in Bamberg Cathedral. It is also the most sinister. All the darkness, mystery and awful power of a vast forest seem concentrated in this majestic head of leaves. The Bamberg leaf mask is a Prince of Darkness.

In the Green Man carvings of the thirteenth, fourteenth and fifteenth centuries the association between the human and plant elements is often suggested as an uneasy or actually hostile relationship rather than as a balanced symbiosis. Sometimes the leaves appear parasitic, drawing their strength from the wretched, emaciated head which bears them. They may seem like a morbid growth and blind the Green Man's eyes with a cataract-like membrane or, even more horribly, sprout from the pupils of the eyes. An example of this macabre feature occurs at Ottery St.Mary in Devon, one of the best of all the English counties

116

for studying variations on the Green Man theme.
There are at least seventeen Green Men in Exeter
Cathedral, but it is in the country churches as,
for example, at Sampford Courtenay, South Tawton,
Spreyton, Ugborough and Widecombe-in-the-Moor,
that the most curious mutants appear. The carvings
sometimes reflect limitations of technique, but the
occasional crudity is more than compensated for by
the liveliness and originality of the ideas. The
making of Green Men would seem to have been something of a folk art in these parts, and to observe
the many variations is like hearing an old folk-
song sung, not in unison, but by different singers,
one after the other, each adding a new verse as he
makes it up on the spot.

It is, of course, necessary for the purposes of
serious study to record more material than can be
found in any one county or any one country, and
besides England, France and Germany have provided
the richest fields for research. Once, however, a
comprehensive collection of photographic records
has been assembled it is possible to show that
almost all the strands of the antique tradition
(for example, the frown, the baleful glare, the
look of grim foreboding, the intensely introspect-
ive expression, the squint, even the little ridge
of flesh above the bridge of the nose — but not
the horn of plenty) and many strands of the early
medieval tradition (for example, the leaves growing out of the nose, the sticking out tongue, the
tricephalos and occasionally some cat or lion-like
features) reappear in the foliate heads of the
later Middle Ages, and as the different strands
are variously selected and variously combined new
shades of meaning are achieved. Many quite new
ideas are picked up and added to modify, or empha-
sise, the meaning.

It is possible that Jack-in-the-Green was among
the many ideas picked up, though I have no con-
clusive evidence for this. I find more allusions

to death and damnation than to life and prosperity
in the medieval leaf heads. The frequent appearance of the motif on tombs and memorials, (a use
continued long after it had fallen out of favour
as an ornament in church architecture), might
suggest the idea of resurrection — a life out of
death symbol — [29] but could equally well suggest:
'For all flesh is as grass and all the glory of
man as the flower of grass. The grass withereth,
and the flower thereof falleth away' Peter,1.24,
and this idea is more consistent with the meaning
of the leaf mask in the early Middle Ages. The
suggestion that the Green Man came to represent
some aspect of residual paganism in the community
seems doubtful. Though pagan in origin, the motif
was developed within the church and was rarely
used in a secular context before the sixteenth
century. I have, however, recorded one notable
exception: a gold harness ornament with a cross-
eyed leaf mask on it. This 'horse-brass', made in
Limoges in the thirteenth century, is now in the
Cluny Museum in Paris. Was the leaf mask used as a
charm, perhaps against the Evil Eye, in the Middle
Ages? Undoubtedly, however, the principal function
of the Green Man in the Church was to serve as an
ornament. The motif is a variant form of leaf
ornament and it was sometimes used simply as an
ornament without any deeper meaning attached to it.
We can find evidence for this in the remarkably
imaginative (and almost imaginary) 'Green Man' in
the porch of St.Mary's, Great Shelford, near Cambridge. It is just, but only just,possible to
recognise a 'face' in the configuration of two
large oak leaves. The 'mouth' is represented by
the space between the proximal leaf lobes and the
crossed leaf stalks, and the 'nose' by a single
acorn. The narrow eye-slits appear in the sinuses
of the leaf lobes. It is a delightful 'now you see
it, now you don't' fantasy. It is, however, pure
ornament.

It seems possible that it was because it could be regarded mainly as a leaf ornament that it was found acceptable in at least one Cistercian Abbey as early as the thirteenth century, as at Kloster Ebrach, in Upper Bavaria, where two leaf masks are used on the portal. Most of the decoration consists of pure foliage, on panels round the portal and on bosses on the inner arches. The leaf masks are apparently introduced to vary the ornament. One of them, which is placed on the keystone, is similar in style to the 'male medusa mask' as it was used in Hellenistic scroll ornament, but with oak leaves replacing acanthus. The other, which is carved on a boss, is also an oak leaf mask. The face is extremely emaciated and seems to have been sucked dry by the greedy leaves growing on it. The expression suggests bitter disillusionment and if any meaning can be attached to this ornament it must refer to sin and death:

So here's a thought your teeth should clench:
'All greenness comes to withering'.

This quotation, from a thirteenth century poem[30] could just as well apply to the Green Man at Fountains, where my quest began. It fits him exactly. I could have read the message at the first glance, but I could not understand how the Green Man could have picked up such a meaning until I had learned to see him in historical perspective and could place him in the framework of tradition.

I cannot refer here to more than a few of the many foliate heads I have hunted and photographed, nor tell more than the bare outline of the Green Man story. Each Green Man tells his own long story, but we can understand it only so far as we are able to pick up the cross-references it contains. I have attempted to trace some of them but many loose ends remain, as I have indicated, and the quest is not ended. It has, however, become more clearly defined as I have learned to ask always,

What are the roots that clutch,
    What branches grow
Out of this stony rubbish?[31]

6. PROTECTIVE SYMBOLS IN THE HOME

Christina Hole

THE STRONG NEED which house-dwellers of every type,
and in every century, have always felt to protect
their homes and those who lived in them against
every form of evil and misfortune, both material
and spiritual, that threatened them has left a
variety of curious traces in many old houses still
standing, or only recently demolished, and in some
domestic habits once, or still, associated with
human dwellings and the stables and outbuildings
attached to them. From time immemorial, every man
who built or maintained a house, to be a lasting
home and refuge for his family, had to guard that
house, as best he could, against the perils of
fire and lightning-stroke, disease and pestilence,
storm, flood, and land-subsidence — and against
the still more dangerous, if less clearly defined,
effects of the Evil Eye, or the actions of demons
and witches. Of the ceremonies and amulets in
which he once trusted, recognisable traces exist
in many half-remembered superstitions, and in
certain symbolic objects still vaguely regarded in
a number of districts as being of protective
significance.

The commonest house-amulet known in this
country — and in practically every other region
where the shod horse is known — is the *Horseshoe*,
nailed singly, or in sets of three or five or
seven, over the threshold of a house or stable
door. It is also a talisman, inasmuch as it is
widely regarded as a luck-bringer, especially if
it is an old shoe found by chance in the roadway.
In the days of horse-traffic, such a find was
probably easy enough, but nowadays it must be
rare, and the more valuable in consequence. It
must be hung the right way up, though which is the
right way and which the wrong — that is, with the

121

points upwards or downwards — remains a matter of debate. The source of the Horseshoe's protective power is commonly said to be threefold: the fact that it is a lunar symbol, resembling in its shape the young, horned crescent moon; that it is associated with the horse, which is itself a symbol of fertility; and that, in addition to all this, it is made of Iron.

Iron, of course, has been credited with the power of warding off evil by people all over the world, since the far-off days when it was a new metal. In its meteorite form, it was heaven-born, and came from the sky surrounded by an aura of mystery and taboo which it never quite lost. When Iron tools and weapons first came into use, their superiority over their stone or bronze prede-cessors was so striking that they, and the smiths who made them, easily became objects of super-stitious awe, especially amongst peoples who were slow to adopt the use of the new metal. In the Middle Ages and later, Iron was believed to keep fairies and evil spirits from the house, and to deflect the spells of witches, and the first and most dangerous glances of the Evil Eye.

Until comparatively recently, a knife thrust into the woodwork of a cradle, or a poker laid across it, protected the baby from being stolen and replaced by a changeling. Aubrey remarks in his *Remaines* that 'In Herefordshire (and those parts), when it thunders and lightenes, the woemen doe putt Iron, e.g. an Iron barr or the like, on the Barrel, to keep the Beer from sowring';[1] and so they did in many districts much later than Aubrey's time. In our own day, housewives not in-frequently place a poker upright against the bars of the grate, so forming a cross, to make the fire burn up brightly when it is sulky. Scientists assure us that this has no effect whatever; but the fact remains that it *appears* to have some effect, as I know from experience — and there are some who attempt to explain the mystery rationally by saying that the upright poker divides the draught, and so makes the chimney draw better.

On the outer walls of some old houses and barns large *Spiral Irons* are often to be seen, usually S-shaped, like a great S falling on its side. Frequently two of these are crossed over each other, in such a way as to present the rough image of a Swastika with curved ends. Some are plain crosses, straight, or slanting in the St.Andrew tradition, but the single S, or the Swastika shapes, are far more common. The function of these *Spiral Irons* is to act as a tie, or lock, to the tie-beam; but because they resemble the Hammer of Thor, they have acquired a symbolical meaning.[2] They are, or were, quite widely explained as a device to defend the house against lightning-stroke, by the use of the Thunder-God's own sign.

Another curious form of domestic fire-insurance, rarely, if ever seen now, but once well-known in country districts, especially in the English Midlands, was the *Lucky Hand*, otherwise known as *St. John's Hand*. It bore the latter name because it had to be prepared on St.John's Eve — June 23rd — and because its virtues were supposed to be derived from the power of St.John the Baptist. He, of course, is one of the greatest saints of the Church, of whose existence and true sanctity no question could ever be raised, even by the most iconoclastic of modern liturgical reformers. He came, as we all know, to prepare the way of the Lord, and to bring sinners to repentance, and was himself a man of extreme austerity. Yet in folk-tradition he has always been associated with the pagan fire-festival of Midsummer, and the ominous Turn of the Year at the Summer Solstice.

From the fifth century onwards, his Feast-Day has been celebrated on June 24th, which is Mid-summer Day, the anniversary on which formerly — and in some places still — great bonfires were lit

123

to strengthen the sun and drive away evil, flaming
wheels were rolled down hillsides, and the saint's
own golden flower, St.John's Wort — which is
quite clearly a. sun-symbol — was brought indoors
to promote good fortune, and protect the house
from fire.

The *Hand* served the same good purpose. On St.
John's Eve, a root of Male Fern was dug up, and
all but five of the unrolled fronds were cut away,
so that what remained looked uncommonly like a
rough, gnarled hand with hooked fingers. It was
then smoked and hardened in one of the ceremonial
Midsummer bonfires, and after being so treated,
became extremely tough and long-lasting. Such a
Hand was often kept for many years, hidden away in
some secret corner of the house; and for so long
as it remained there, that house was believed to
be safe from the peril of fire, and from a variety
of other misfortunes.[3]

Salt — which is itself incorruptible and pre-
serves other things from decay — is a symbol of
immortality and of truth, sacred alike in pagan
and in Christian times. In the old Norse form of
baptism, a pinch of *salt* was placed in the child's
mouth, and today it is often used in our own
baptismal chrism.[4] In Derbyshire, until recently,
oaths were sometimes taken upon *salt*, instead of
on the Bible.[5] Old houses in East Anglia often had
their chimneys lined with salt-glazed bricks, to
keep away evil influences.[6] It is still not unusual for a plate of salt to be set upon a corpse
as soon as death has occurred, or failing that,
for a pail of salt-and-water to be put under the
bed. The customary explanation today is that it
prevents the body from swelling, but originally it
had another meaning. Like the candles which burnt
round the bed, it protected the dead man from the
demons who were believed to cluster round the soul
at the moment of death, and in the days immediately following.

A curious example of the way folklore grows was told to me a few years ago by a Staffordshire woman.[7] Her father was a doctor who possessed a fine collection of old pewter plates. After a death in the neighbourhood, he was quite frequently asked by the dead man's relatives to lend one of these plates — to hold the *death-salt*. On asking why one of their own china plates would not do, he was usually told that the salt would 'work' more efficaciously if it lay upon metal. Presumably, it normally did so in the seventeenth century, when pewter was a customary table-ware; but — except for possible vague memories of this fact — there does not seem to be any established tradition to account for this odd local belief.

At the other end of life, a new-born baby was often given a pinch or a handful of salt during the dangerous period between birth and baptism. Other traditional gifts at this time were small silver coins — usually a sixpence — an egg, and a box of matches, which symbolised fire and, like the salt, protected the unchristened child from witchcraft and other perils.

Salt, too, is still one of the gifts which the First Foot in Scotland and Northern England brings with him when he comes to a house in the early hours of New Year's Day. Bread and coal, salt or money are the usual gifts, symbolising food and warmth, safety and prosperity all through the coming year. In Scotland, there is often a bottle of whiskey as well — but perhaps we need not explore very deeply into the mysteries of symbolism to account for that. The First Foot himself is the new-born year, and what he brings, and how he looks, foretell what is to come. First-footing is a gay ceremony — more of a frolic than anything else — but the old rules are still generally observed. For a house to go unvisited in a district where the custom is kept up, or for the First Foot, when he does come, to be the wrong

sort of man, is a very bad omen. He should be
young, if possible, and anyway, vigorous and
healthy; he should not be flat-footed, or cross-
eyed, nor should his eyebrows meet across his nose.
He must be dark-haired or dark-complexioned in
most areas, though in a few districts the opposite
rule prevails, and he must be fair. Ideally, he
should be a stranger — unknown to those he visits,
as the new year is still unknown; but since the
number of dark-haired strangers at large in the
middle of a winter night, and bearing suitable
gifts in their hands, is never very great, the
First Foot usually turns out to be a friend, or at
least, a resident of the town or village concerned.
The one thing he must never be is a woman of any
colour, for that would be most unlucky. Folklore,
as yet, knows nothing of Women's Lib.

The *Evil Eye* does not seem to have been so
widely feared in England as in some Mediterranean
countries, where the dread of it still flourishes.[8]
In Italy, charms and amulets of various kinds, including the *'horned hand'*, with the index and
little fingers extended, and the other fingers and
thumb clenched, or the crescent moon with a man's
face between the horns, are frequently worn to
protect the wearer. Once these amulets were commonly made of silver because that is the metal of
Diana; nowadays, they are more usually made of
plastic. In Malta and Corfu, and some parts of
Spain, *cattle-horns*[9] are often set up on the
fronts of houses, and sometimes indoors as well,
singly, or in pairs, or attached to the painted
skulls of animals. Their function is to catch the
first glance of the possibly evil-eyed visitor, or
passer-by, before he has time to look at anything
else — and allow its dangers to slip along the
horns, and away into the air, like lightning
running down a lightning-conductor.

In England, when some unfortunate person believed himself, or his animals, to be overlooked,

a witch — known or unknown — was usually blamed.
Sometimes, however, the misfortune was ascribed to
some man or woman who possessed the *Evil Eye*. Such
a person was not necessarily a witch, though he
might be that as well. No one can be a witch without his own consent and wish, but the *Evil Eye* may
be an involuntary affliction. Whoever had it might
not be at all evilly disposed as far as his
character went, but there was a deadly power in
his eyes which brought misfortune to whatever
person or thing he steadily regarded. In their
book, *About Yorkshire*, published in 1883, Thomas
and Katherine MacQuoid mentioned a well-inten-
tioned individual at Fyling Thorpe who never
looked at anyone to whom he spoke, and went about
with his eyes fixed on the ground, for fear of
harming some innocent passer-by. The first glance
was the most dangerous, and especially the first
glance of the morning; another Yorkshire story relates how one man in Craven used to look first at
a pear-tree outside his house, and never went
where he was likely to encounter some human being
or animal until he had done so. The tree withered
slowly, and eventually died.

In a Somerset village known to me between the
two Wars of our time, there was a midwife who was
believed to have the *Evil Eye*. Hers might have
been thought a rather unfortunate profession for
anyone so afflicted, but the local women employed
her for their confinements, nevertheless, because
they were afraid of offending her. Had they done
so, she had only to turn the power of her eyes
upon them, or their children, to obtain her
revenge; but there is no record known to me of her
ever having done so. She continued in active
practice until she retired of her own accord,
through old age; and thereafter she lived on
peacefully in the neighbourhood until she died in
1945.

Small pebbles or flints, with a natural hole in

127

them, which are known as *Hag-stones*, or sometimes
as Witch-stones or Mare-stones, were supposed to
be amulets against the *Evil Eye*, probably because
they so often resemble the rough image of an Eye,
the hole serving as the pupil. The *Eye* is a very
ancient protective symbol, representing the All-
Seeing Eye of God; in Egyptian tradition, it was
the *Eye of Horus*, which denoted fertility, far-
sightedness, and immunity from bodily harm. The
Eye painted on the prow of some Mediterranean
fishing-boats is said to be the *Eye of Horus*,
though it is not always recognised as such by the
fishermen today.[10]

A *Hag-stone* hung upon the inside of the door,
or attached to the iron door-key, preserved the
house from the blighting influence of the *Evil Eye*
and the inroads of witches or fairies. Worn on the
person, or hung over the bedhead, it kept off
nightmares and rheumatism, and various other
diseases. Farmers used to hang such stones in
their stables and cow-byres to save the horses
from night-sweats, and prevent witches from stealing the milk of cows. Besides averting these
particular ills, the presence of a *Hag-stone* was
also supposed to promote the general health and
welfare of the animals.

A large perforated flint was once kept at
Dixies Farm, at Ashwell in Hertfordshire, suspended from the rafters of the stables. In 1850, the
stables were burnt down, along with several other
outbuildings. The flint was rescued, but for some
reason it was not immediately hung up again in
the new stables, when these were built. Some years
later, three horses died of the disease known as
Glanders, and on the advice of a horse-dealer, re-
course was had once more to the power of the *Hag-
stone*. It was rehung, and was never taken down
again until 1952. By then, the farm had been
mechanised, and there were no horses left. The
Curator of the Ashwell Village Museum asked the

owner to lend the amulet to the Museum, and his
request was granted, on two conditions. One was
that someone unconnected with the farm should be
sent to take it down, because no one at Dixies was
willing to do so. The other was that if the removal was followed by any misfortune, either to
the farm itself or to any of its inhabitants, it
should be brought back at once, and rehung in its
old place in the now-empty stables.[11]

Animal-bones are often found in the walls or
foundations of old houses, and are usually attributed to lingering memories of foundation
sacrifice, though there may be other explanations
for their presence. Horse-bones, and sometimes
horse-skulls, have been discovered in houses of
various sizes in many parts of Britain, including
one at Bungay, in Suffolk, where some forty skulls
were found neatly laid under the floor in a sort
of pattern. In another, at Littleport, in Cambridgeshire, there was a layer of animal-bones
in the chimney. Elsewhere ox, or sheep, or horse
bones have occurred under hearth-stones, or
tightly packed between joists, or in the roof. In
the White Horse Inn, in Bedford (now demolished),
there was a dried rat preserved in the wall.

One explanation for the skulls under floors is
that they were put there to improve the acoustical
effects of places where people sang or danced, or
where threshing took place, to make the floors
bend better to meet the flail.[12] But this utili-
tarian purpose may not have been the only one. In
The Pattern Under the Plough,[13] George Ewart Evans
mentions an account he received from a Yorkshire
informant concerning the village of Halton East,
where horse-skulls were found under the flagstones
of some cottages then being restored. This man
said there was a local tradition there that, when
a good horse died, its head was buried in order to
retain some of its virtues, and to protect the
house from evil. In other words, it was used as a

protective amulet — and the fact that *images of animals*, especially horses, were often carved on the ridge-tiles of medieval houses suggests that some such idea may have been held once in more places than Halton East.

7. SYMBOLS IN FAIRY TALES

Katharine M.Briggs

IT IS EASY to claim almost anything for a symbol,
and indeed in groping through Jung's secret language of the Unconscious it is hard to find any
object, action or concept in an emotionally
charged dream which cannot be symbolically interpreted. The same holds good in pictures, especially in Surrealist ones and in evocative
poetry. The game of Hunt the Symbol is a fascinating one, and not too difficult to play. I have
lately acquired a Symposium on Symbols edited by
Dr.Jung[1] and lavishly illustrated in a style
suited to my rather blunt and unsophisticated
intelligence, and have listed in it a number of
symbols which occur freely in fairy tales. It has
been suggested that those implements which were
new and startling inventions to Primitive Man became loaded with magical significance; mirrors,
combs, spindles, cauldrons, wrought metal, wheels
and even brooms have perhaps borrowed magical
properties from their aboriginal strangeness. It
is conceivable that their original numinousness
together with their long habitation in the human
mind made them appropriate words in the language
of symbol as well as appropriate vehicles for
magic. At least I think I may say that many of the
enchanted implements, elements and creatures of
fairy tales are well recognised symbols in their
naturalistic form.

Let us begin with a few artifacts which have
magical power in their own right and are endowed
with magical power in fairy tales. First, for
those made of metal: — iron or steel and gold are
the commonest metals in fairy tales, and a sword
is perhaps most often mentioned. It will be sim-
plest to recount a few stories to illustrate the
use of these magical symbols and I have chosen

stories in which the symbols cluster fairly
thickly, so that I can refer back to them without
having to tell too many. The magical sword most
often mentioned is the *Sword of Sharpness*, such as
that which Athene gave to Perseus, and which is to
be found in many fairy stories.

. As a first example let us take the Chapbook
version of Jack the Giant Killer, known as Jack
and the Giants.[2] This is of special interest
because it is a thinly disguised example of the
tale of the Grateful Dead (Type 506), well-known
in Celtic areas of Britain but rare in England. It
must once have been well-known here, for it is
told entire in Peele's *Old Wives' Tale* where the
dead man is called Jack. In this Chapbook the
direct connection between Jack and the ransomed
corpse is lost, otherwise the tale is complete.

King Arthur's only son desired of his father to
furnish him with a certain sum of money, that he
might go and seek his fortune in the principal-
ity of Wales, where a beautiful Lady lived, whom
he heard was possessed with seven evil spirits;
but the King his father advised him utterly
against it, yet he would not be persuaded of it;
so that he granted what he requested, which was
one horse loaded with money, and another for
himself to ride on; thus he went forth without
any attendants.

Now after several days' travel, he came to a
market-town in Wales, where he beheld a large
concourse of people gathered together; the
King's son demanded the reason of it, and was
told that they arrested a corpse for many large
sums of money, which the deceased owed when he
died. The King's son replied, 'It is a pity
that creditors should be so cruel. Go bury the
dead,' said he, 'and let his creditors come to
my lodging and their debts shall be discharged.'
Accordingly they came, and in such great numbers

132

that before night he had almost left himself
moneyless.

Now Jack-the-Giant-Killer being there, and seeing the generosity of the King's son, he was
taken with him, and desired to be his servant;
it was agreed upon, and the next morning they
set forward, when, riding out at the town-end,
an old woman called after him, crying out, 'He
hath owed me twopence these five years; pray sir,
pay me as well as the rest!' He put his hand
into his pocket, and gave it her; it being the
last he had left, the King's son turning to Jack,
said, 'I cannot tell how I will subsist in my
intended journey.' 'For that,' quoth Jack, 'take
you no thought nor care. Let me alone, I warrant
you we will not want.'

Now Jack, having a small spell in his pocket,
which served at noon to give them a refreshment,
when done, they had not one penny left betwixt
them; the afternoon they spent in travel and
familiar discourse, till the sun began to grow
low, at which time the King's son said, 'Jack,
since we have no money, where can we think to
lodge this night?' Jack replied, 'Master, we'll
do well enough, for I have an uncle lives within
two little miles of this; he's a huge and monstrous giant with three heads: he'll fight five
hundred men in armour, and make them to fly before him.' 'Alas,' quoth the King's son, 'what
shall we do there? He'll certainly chop us both
up at one mouthful! nay, we are scarce enough
to fill one of his hollow teeth.' 'It is no
matter for that,' quoth Jack, 'I myself will go
before, and prepare the way for you: therefore
tarry here, and wait my return.'

He waits, and Jack rides full speed, when coming
to the gates of the Castle, he knocked with such
a force, that he made all the neighbouring hills

133

to resound. The giant with a voice like thunder, roared out, 'Who's there?' He answered, 'None but your poor cousin Jack.' Quoth he, 'What news with my poor cousin Jack?' He replied, 'Dear uncle, heavy news, God wot.' 'Prithee, what heavy news can come to me? I am a giant with three heads, and besides thou knowest I can fight five hundred men in armour, and make them fly like chaff before the wind.' 'O! but,' quoth Jack, 'here's the King's son coming with a thousand men in armour to kill you, and so to destroy all that you have!' 'Oh! cousin Jack, this is heavy news indeed: I have a large vault under the ground, where I will immediately hide myself, and thou shalt lock, bolt, and bar me in, and keep the keys till the King's son is gone.'

Now Jack having secured the giant, he soon returned and fetched his master, they were both heartily merry with the wine, and other dainties which were in the house: so that night they rested in very pleasant lodgings, while the poor uncle, the giant, lay trembling in the vault underground.

Early in the morning, Jack furnished his master with a fresh supply of gold and silver, and then set him three miles forward on his journey, concluding he was then pretty well out of the smell of the giant, and then returned to let his uncle out of the hole, who asked Jack what he would give him in reward if his castle was not demolished. 'Why,' quoth Jack, 'I desire nothing but the old coat and cap, together with this old rusty sword and slippers, which are at your bedhead.' Quoth the giant, 'Thou shalt have them, and pray keep them for my sake, for they are things of excellent use. The coat will keep you invisible, the cap will furnish you with knowledge, the sword cuts in sunder whatever you

134

strike, and the shoes are of extraordinary
swiftness; these may be serviceable to you, and
therefore pray take them with all my heart.'
Jack takes them, thanking his uncle, and follows
his master.

Jack having overtaken his master, they soon
after arrived at the Lady's house, who finding
the King's son to be a suitor, she prepared a
banquet for him, which being ended, she wiped
his mouth with her handkerchief, saying, 'You
must shew me this one to-morrow morning, or else
lose your head': and with that she put it into
her bosom.

The King's son went to bed very sorrowful, but
Jack's cap of knowledge instructed him how to
obtain it. In the middle of the night, she
called on her familiar spirit to carry her to
her friend Lucifer. Jack soon put on his coat of
darkness with his shoes of swiftness, and was
there as soon as her; by reason of his coat they
could not see him. When she entered the place
she gave the handkerchief to Old Lucifer, who
laid it upon a shelf; from whence Jack took, and
brought it to his master, who shewed it to the
lady next day, and so saved his life.

The next night she saluted the King's son, telling him he must show her to-morrow morning the
lips that she kissed last, this night, or else
lose his head. 'Ah,' replied he, 'if you kiss
none but mine, I will': ''tis neither here nor
there,' said she, 'if you do not death's your
portion.' At midnight she went as before, and
was angry with Lucifer for letting the handkerchief go: 'But now,' said she, 'I will be too
hard for the King's son, for I will kiss thee,
and he's to shew thy lips,' which she did; Jack
standing near him with his sword of sharpness,
cut off the devil's head, and brought it under

135

his invisible coat to his master, who was in bed, and laid it at the end of his bolster. In the morning, when the lady came up, he pulled it out by the horns, and shewed her the devil's lips which she kissed last.

Thus, having answered her twice, the enchantment broke, and the evil spirits left her; at which time she appeared in all her beauty, a beautiful and virtuous creature. They were married the next morning in great pomp and solemnity, and soon after they returned with a numerous company to the court of King Arthur, where they were received with the greatest joy, and loud acclamations by the whole court. Jack, for the many and great exploits he had done for the good of his country, was made one of the Knights of the Round Table.

Here are most of the motifs to be found in The Grateful Dead;[3] E.341.I (Corpse is being held unburied, hero pays debt and secures burial of corpse); H.322.I (Suitor test: finding object hidden by princess); T.118 (Girl enamoured of a monster) and T.172.2.1 (Grateful dead man kills princess's monster husband).[4] The missing motifs M.241 (Bargain to divide all winnings) and M.241.1 (Half the bride demanded) are found in *The Old Wives' Tale*[5] and Campbell's 'Barra Widow's Son'[6] and in Douglas Hyde's 'The King of Ireland's Son',[7] though in this tale the Bargain is for the first kiss of the bride, whose poison is drawn out of her by the Short Green Man. Hans Anderson's 'Travelling Companion' is on the same theme.[8]

A sword was a necessary property for magicians and elaborate instructions for their sanctification are to be found in 'The Key of Solomon'[9] and other magical manuscripts. Sometimes swords have magical qualities in their own right through the strength of cold iron against enchantment. In two very different Grimm stories, 'The Three

Little Men in the Wood'[10] and 'The King's Son Who
Feared Nothing'[11] an evil spell is broken by
swinging a sword three times over the enchanted
object. The sword by which Child Rowland won his
victory over the Elf King had perhaps some special
qualities, for it was his father's claymore that
never struck in vain, girded on with special
solemnity by his Mother.[12] The story may not be
known to all of you, and as it is one of the best
of our English Fairy Tales and was quoted by
Shakespeare, I will tell it you briefly. It is
from Jamieson's *Northern Antiquities* and was told
to Jamieson when he was about eight years old by
an old tailor who worked in his father's house. It
is a cante Fable with verse and prose interspersed.

Child Rowland and his two brothers were playing
at the ball, and there was their sister Burd Ellen
in the midst among them all.

'Child Rowland kicked it wi' his foot,
    And keepit it wi' his knee:
And ay, as he play'd out o'er them a'
    O'er the kirk he gar'd it flee.

'Burd Ellen round about the aisle
    to seek the ba' is gane:
But they bade lang and ay langer,
    And she camena back again.

'They sought her east, they sought her west,
    They sought her up and down;
And wae were the hearts (in merry Carlisle)
    For she was nae gait found!'

At last the eldest brother got leave from his
mother to seek for Burd Ellen, and she told him to
go to the Warlock Merlin and get reid from him
what he should do. Merlin told him that Burd Ellen
had been carried off by the King of Elfland to his
Dark Tower. It was hard to win there and harder
yet to win back, but he told him every last thing
he must do, and the Eldest Brother set out. But he

137

never came back. After a weary while the second
Brother set out; but he never came back, and at
length Child Rowland fleeched and prayed at his
Mother to let him go too. It was a hard leave to
get, but she granted it at last and she girt about
him his father's good claymore that never struck
in vain and told him to obey every word that
Warlock Merlin told him. So he went to Merlin, and
Merlin told him as he told his brothers the way he
must go to reach Elfland, and that once he got
there he must cut off the head of everyone that
would speak to him until he reached Burd Ellen,
and once he was in Elfland he must bite no bit and
drink no drop if he ever hoped to see Middle Earth
again. So Child Rowland set out and he went on and
further on until he got to Elfland, and the first
man he saw there was the King of Elfland's horseherd, and he asked him how to get to the Dark
Tower, and the horseherd told him to go on to the
cowherd who might know. So Child Rowland drew his
father's good claymore that never struck in vain
and struck off the horseherd's head, and so on to
the cowherd and the sheepherd and many more till
he got to the henwife, and each one he served as
he had served the first. The henwife showed him a
green hill ringed with terraces, and told him to
go three times round it widdershins and each time
to say: 'Open door! Open door! and let me come in!'
And he smote off her head too and did as she had
said, and at the third time round a door opened in
the dark hill, and he went into the jewelled
palace of the King of Elfland. In the great room
in the middle of it Burd Ellen was sitting combing
her yellow hair with a silver comb and she burst
out with grief at seeing him,

'And hear ye this, my youngest brither,
  Why badena ye at hame?
Had ye a hunder and thousand lives,
  Ye canna brook ane o' them.'

138

But Child Rowland told her he had come to take her
home, and they talked long together till at the
end he grew faint with hunger and asked her to
bring him food. She was bespelled and had no power
to warn him, so she fetched him a golden bowl of
bread and milk, and he raised it to his lips and
saw her looking so sadly at him that he remembered
Merlin's words and cried out, 'I will neither
taste nor touch until I free you from Elfland.'
And as he flung the bowl on the floor the great
folding doors burst open and he heard the King of
Elfland crying

'With fi, fi, fo, and fum!
I smell the blood of a Christian man!
Be he dead, be he living, wi' my brand
I'll clash his barns frae his barn-pan!'

Then Child Rowland flashed out his father's good
claymore that never struck in vain, and up and
down the hall of Elfland they fought till he got
the Elf King down and promised him death unless he
brought his two brothers back to life and set him
and Burd Ellen free. So the King of Elfland drew
out a crystal phial full of a bright red oil, and
he touched the lips and nostrils and eyes and
finger-tips of the two brothers, and they started
up as well as they had ever been, and all went
home to the Queen their Mother in merry Carlisle.

Jacobs, who retells the story, suggests plaus-
ibly that Burd Ellen was carried away because she
went widdershins the church, and certainly Child
Rowland went widdershins the enchanted hill as
anyone must do who wants to get into Elfland.

A dirk often serves the same purpose as a sword
because it is made of cold iron. It was by a dirk
that the Smith in Campbell's tale of 'The Smith and
the Fairies'[13] held a door open to rescue his son
out of the fairy hill. At the time of the full
moon it rose on columns, and he stuck his dirk
into the door by which he entered, protected by a

Bible and a cock. When the fairies saw him they
tried to shut down the hill and keep him prisoner
too, but the door which was protected by the dirk
could not be closed. The Bible protected him from
attacks, and when the racket waked the drowsy cock
so that it struggled to his shoulder and crowed
the fairies scattered to the dark corners of the
hill and the smith was able to seize his boy and
take him out. There are various symbols here, the
power of the Holy Word and the sun-loving bird,
symbol of the day which is feared by the creatures
of darkness, as well as the cold iron. Often people
who ventured among fairies or devils were advised
to take salt with them as well, but there are
enough symbols of power here to serve the Smith's
turn.

A horseshoe is another metal artifact of great
potency, but it occurs more in Legend than in
Fairy Tales.

Gold is a Sun symbol in itself, and has an
extra quality because it is untarnishable. In the
Great Chain of Being[14] gold was the highest and
purest metal, and therefore had various symbolical
uses, to represent royalty and pre-eminence, and
perhaps above all to represent chastity. You
probably all recall the opening of 'Tam Lin':[15]

'O I forbid you, maiden a',
That wear gowd on your hair,
To come or gae to Carterhaugh,
For young Tam Lin is there.'

This has been interpreted not to indicate
wealth but maiden chastity.[16] In the same way the
ball in 'The Frog Prince', Grimm No.1 — has been
interpreted as a symbol of maidenhead, though
other versions of the type, such as 'The Paddo'[17]
do not mention a ball at all. In Grimm's 'Iron
Hans'[18] and the tale of 'Elidorus and the Golden
Ball'[19] the ball cannot be interpreted as a symbol
of virginity. There is one story, however, that

seems to bear out the contention — the English
tale of 'The Golden Ball'.[20]

There were two lasses, daughters of one mother,
and as they came from the fair, they saw a right
bonny young man stand at the house-door before
them. They never saw such a bonny man before. He
had gold on his cap, gold on his finger, gold on
his neck, a red gold watch-chain — eh! but he
had brass. He had a golden ball in each hand. He
gave a ball to each lass, and she was to keep it,
and if she lost it, she was to be hanged. One of
the lasses, 'twas the youngest, lost her ball.
I'll tell thee how. She was by a park-paling,
and she was tossing her ball, and it went up,
and up, and up, till it went fair over the pal-
ing; and when she climbed up to look, the ball
ran along the green grass, and it went right
forward to the door of the house, and the ball
went in and she saw it no more.

So she was taken away to be hanged by the
neck till she was dead because she'd lost her
ball.

But she had a sweetheart, and he said he
would go and get the ball. So he went to the
park-gate, but 'twas shut; so he climbed the
hedge, and when he got to the top of the hedge,
an old woman rose up out of the dyke before him,
and said, if he wanted to get the ball, he must
sleep three nights in the house. He said he would.

Then he went into the house, and looked for
the ball, but could not find it. Night came on
and he heard bogles move in the courtyard; so he
looked out o' the window, and the yard was full
of them.

Presently he heard steps coming upstairs. He
hid behind the door, and was as still as a mouse.
Then in came a big giant five times as tall as

141

he, and the giant looked round but did not see
the lad, so he went to the window and bowed to
look out; and as he bowed on the elbows to see
the bogles in the yard, the lad stepped behind
him, and with one blow of his sword he cut him
in twain, so that the top part of him fell in
the yard, and the bottom part stood looking out
of the window.

There was a great cry from the bogles when
they saw half the giant come tumbling down to
them, and they called out, 'There comes half our
master, give us the other half.'

So the lad said, 'It's no use of thee, thou
pair of legs, standing alone at the window, as
thou hast no eye to see with, so go join thy
brother'; and he cast the lower part of the
giant after the top part. Now when the bogles
had gotten all the giant they were quiet.

Next night the lad was at the house again,
and now a second giant came in at door, and as
he came in the lad cut him in twain, but the
legs walked on to the chimney and went up it.
'Go, get thee after thy legs,' said the lad to
the head, and he cast the head up the chimney
too.

The third night the lad got into bed, and he
heard the bogles striving under the bed, and
they had the ball there, and they were casting
it to and fro.

Now one of them has his leg thrust out from
under bed, so the lad brings his sword down and
cuts it off. Then another thrusts his arm out at
other side of the bed, and the lad cuts that off.
So at last he had maimed them all, and they all
went crying and wailing off, and forgot the ball,
but he took it from under the bed, and went to
seek his truelove.

The tale continues with a version of 'The Maid
Freed from the Gallows', best known in the folk-
song of 'The Briery Bush'.[21] It goes through a
catalogue of her relations, her mother, her father,
her brother, her sister and so on till we come to:

'Stop, stop; I see my sweetheart coming!
Sweetheart, hast brought my golden ball
And come to set me free?'
'Aye, I have brought thy golden ball
And come to set thee free.
I have not come to see thee hung
Upon this gallows tree.'

The three nights spent in a haunted house as a
means of disenchantment (motif H.1411) occur in a
great many tales, particularly those about a fear-
less boy (type 326).

A golden cup is often used with symbolic sig-
nificance. We have come across one in 'Child Rowland', but here it merely suggests the riches of
Elfland, though fairy gold was often illusory.
Many cups and cauldrons are used in fairy tales
and legends as symbols of plenty or of healing,
the magic cup stolen by the butler in William of
Newridge's *Chronicle*,[22] the Grail cup which would
give to every man the food he most desired, the
Fairy Cauldron at Frensham Church,[23] Medea's
Cauldron of Renewal and the Cauldron in the
Mabingion and some Irish legends in which the dead
were boiled and their life renewed. There need be
no explanation of the significance of a golden
crown; golden rings and indeed rings of all kinds
are of endless significance, from the 'gay gold
ring with seven bright diamonds set therein'[24] by
which Hind Horn could perceive the constancy of
his Princess, to wishing rings and that arm-ring
conferring supernatural strength which was won by
the 'King's Son Who Feared Nothing', Grimm 121. It
is hard to come to an end of them. All apples are
magic and have been used symbolically in the

earliest times, but golden apples have a special
importance. The golden apples and the ring of
power are combined in 'The King's Son Who Feared
Nothing'. I have already referred to the symbolic
use of the sword in this tale, and here too we
have the giant, symbol of mindless power, and the
ritual of silence so often enjoined in tales of
treasure-seeking and in encounters with supernatural creatures as almost to be raised to a
symbol. It is a good tale, not well-known, and I
think it worth the telling.

There was once a king's son, who was no longer
content to stay at home in his father's house,
and as he had no fear of anything, he thought:
'I will go forth into the wide world, there the
time will not seem long to me, and I shall see
wonders enough'. So he took leave of his parents,
and went forth, and on and on from morning till
night, and whichever way his path led it was the
same to him. It came to pass that he arrived at
the house of a giant, and as he was so tired he
sat down by the door and rested. And as he let
his eyes roam here and there, he saw the giant's
playthings lying in the yard. These were a
couple of enormous balls, and nine-pins as tall
as a man. After a while he had a fancy to set
the nine-pins up and then rolled the balls at
them, and screamed and cried out when the nine-
pins fell, and had a merry time of it. The giant
heard the noise, stretched his head out of the
window, and saw a man who was not taller than
other men, and yet played with his nine-pins.
'Little worm,' cried he, 'why are you playing
with my balls? Who gave you strength to do it?'
The King's son looked up, saw the giant, and
said: 'Oh, you blockhead, you think indeed that
you only have strong arms, I can do everything I
want to do.' The giant came down and watched the
bowling with great admiration, and said: 'Child
of man, if you are one of that kind, go and

144

bring me an apple of the tree of life.' 'What do you want with it?' said the King's son. 'I do not want the apple for myself,' answered the giant, 'but I have a betrothed bride who wishes for it. I have travelled far about the world and cannot find the tree.' 'I will soon find it,' said the King's son, 'and I do not know what is to prevent me from getting the apple down.' The giant said: 'You really believe it to be so easy! The garden in which the tree stands is surrounded by an iron railing, and in front of the railing lie wild beasts, each close to the other, and they keep watch and let no man go in.' 'They will be sure to let me in,' said the King's son. 'Yes, but even if you do get into the garden, and see the apple hanging to the tree, it is still not yours; a ring hangs in front of it, through which any one who wants to reach the apple and break it off, must put his hand, and no one has yet had the luck to do it.' 'That luck will be mine,' said the King's son.

Then he took leave of the giant, and went forth over mountain and valley, and through plains and forests, until at length he came to the wondrous garden.

The beasts lay round about it, but they had put their heads down and were asleep. Moreover, they did not awake when he went up to them, so he stepped over them, climbed the fence, and got safely into the garden. There, in the very middle of it, stood the tree of life, and the red apples were shining upon the branches. He climbed up the trunk to the top, and as he was about to reach out for an apple, he saw a ring hanging before it; but he thrust his hand through that without any difficulty, and picked the apple. The ring closed tightly on his arm, and all at once he felt a prodigious strength flowing through his veins. When he had come down

again from the tree with the apple, he would not
climb over the fence, but grasped the great gate,
and had no need to shake it more than once before it sprang open with a loud crash. Then he
went out, and the lion which had been lying in
front of the gate, was awake and sprang after
him, not in rage and fierceness, but following
him humbly as its master.

The King's son took the giant the apple he
had promised him, and said: 'You see, I have
brought it without difficulty.' The giant was
glad that his desire had been so soon satisfied,
hastened to his bride, and gave her the apple
for which she had wished. She was a beautiful
and wise maiden, and as she did not see the ring
on his arm, she said: 'I shall never believe
that you have brought the apple, until I see the
ring on your arm.' The giant said: 'I have
nothing to do but go home and fetch it,' and
thought it would be easy to take away by force
from the weak man, what he would not give of his
own free will. He therefore demanded the ring
from him, but the King's son refused it. 'Where
the apple is, the ring must be also,' said the
giant; 'if you will not give it of your own
accord, you must fight me for it.'

They wrestled with each other for a long
time, but the giant could not harm the King's
son, who was strengthened by the magical power
of the ring. Then the giant thought of a ruse,
and said: 'I have got warm with fighting, and so
have you. We will bathe in the river, and cool
ourselves before we begin again.' The King's son,
who knew nothing of falsehood, went with him to
the water, and pulled off with his clothes the
ring also from his arm, and sprang into the
river. The giant instantly snatched the ring,
and ran away with it, but the lion, which had
observed the theft, pursued the giant, tore the

ring out of his hand, and brought it back to its
master. Then the giant placed himself behind an
oak-tree, and while the King's son was busy
putting on his clothes again, surprised him, and
put both his eyes out.

And now the unhappy King's son stood there,
and was blind and knew not how to help himself.
Then the giant came back to him, took him by the
hand as if he were someone who wanted to guide
him, and led him to the top of a high rock.
There he left him standing, and thought: 'Just
two steps more, and he will fall down and kill
himself, and I can take the ring from him.' But
the faithful lion had not deserted its master;
it held him fast by the clothes, and drew him
gradually back again. When the giant came and
wanted to rob the dead man, he saw that his
cunning had been in vain. 'Is there no way, then,
of destroying a weak child of man like that?'
said he angrily to himself, and seized the
King's son and led him back again to the precipice by another way, but the lion which saw his
evil design, helped its master out of danger
here also. When they had come close to the edge,
the giant let the blind man's hand drop, and was
going to leave him behind alone, but the lion
pushed the giant so that he was thrown down and
fell, dashed into pieces, on the ground.

The faithful animal again drew its master
back from the precipice, and guided him to a
tree by which flowed a clear brook. The King's
son sat down there, but the lion lay down, and
sprinkled the water in his face with its paws.
Scarcely had a couple of drops wetted the
sockets of his eyes, than he was once more able
to see something, and noticed a little bird fly-
ing quite close by, which hit itself against the
trunk of a tree. So it went down to the water
and bathed itself therein, and then it soared

147

upwards and swept between the trees without
touching them, as if it had recovered its sight.
Then the King's son recognised a sign from God
and stooped down to the water, and washed and
bathed his face in it. And when he arose he had
his eyes once more, brighter and clearer than
they had ever been.

The King's son thanked God for his great
mercy, and travelled with his lion onwards
through the world. And it came to pass that he
arrived before the castle which was enchanted.
In the gateway stood a maiden of beautiful form
and fine face, but she was quite black. She
spoke to him and said: 'Ah, if you could but
deliver me from the evil spell which is thrown
over me.' 'What shall I do?' said the King's son.
The maiden answered: 'You must pass three nights
in the great hall of this enchanted castle, but
you must let no fear enter your heart. When they
are doing their worst to torment you, if you
bear it without letting a sound escape you, I
shall be free. Your life they dare not take.'
Then said the King's son: 'I have no fear, with
God's help I will try it.' So he went gaily into
the castle, and when it grew dark he seated himself in the large hall and waited. Everything
was quiet however, till midnight, when all at
once a great tumult began, and out of every home
and corner came little devils. They behaved as
if they did not see him, seated themselves in
the middle of the room, lighted a fire, and
began to gamble. When one of them lost, he said:
'It is not right; some one is here who does not
belong to us; it is his fault that I am losing.'
'Wait, you fellow behind the stove, I am coming,'
said the other. The screaming became still
louder, so that no one could have heard it without terror. The King's son stayed sitting quite
calmly, and was not afraid; but at last the
devils jumped up from the ground, and fell on

148

him, and there were so many of them that he
could not defend himself from them. They dragged
him about on the floor, pinched him, pricked him,
beat him, tormented him, but no sound escaped
from him. Towards morning they disappeared, and
he was so exhausted that he could scarcely move
his limbs, but when day dawned the black maiden
came to him. She bore in her hand a little
bottle wherein was the water of life wherewith
she washed him, and he at once felt all pain
depart and new strength flow through his veins.
She said: 'You have held out successfully for
one night, but two more lie before you.' Then
she went away again, and as she was going, he
observed that her feet had become white. The
next night the devils came and began their
gambling anew. They fell on the King's son, and
beat him much more severely than the night before, until his body was covered with wounds.
But as he bore all quietly, they were forced to
leave him, and when dawn appeared, the maiden
came and healed him with the water of life. And
when she went away, he saw with joy that she had
already become white to the tips of her fingers.
And now he had only one night more to go through,
but it was the worst. The devils came again:
'Are you still there?' cried they, 'you shall be
tormented till your breath stops.' They pricked
him and beat him, and threw him here and there,
and pulled him by the arms and legs as if they
wanted to tear him to pieces, but he bore everything, and never uttered a cry. At last the
devils vanished, but he lay fainting there, and
did not stir, nor could he raise his eyes to
look at the maiden who came in, and sprinkled
and bathed him with the water of life. But
suddenly he was freed from all pain, and felt
fresh and healthy as if he had awakened from
sleep, and when he opened his eyes he saw the
maiden standing by him, snow-white, and fair as

day. 'Rise,' said she, 'and swing your sword
three times over the stairs, and then all will
be delivered.' And when he had done that, the
whole castle was released from enchantment, and
the maiden was a rich King's daughter. The
servants came and said that the table was set in
the great hall, and dinner served up. Then they
sat down and ate and drank together, and in the
evening the wedding was solemnized with great
rejoicings.

I don't wish to press the point, but it seems to
me that the last part of this tale may well be a
symbolic version of St.Patrick's Purgatory by
which the black soul is whitened by the steadfast
endurance of suffering.[25]

The magical and symbolical powers of a mirror
almost declare themselves. They were used for
divination and for refraction to throw back the
evil eye, as Perseus' polished shield was used
against the Gorgon or men used a mirror against a
cockatrice, so that it perished by its own poison.
In one of the Dragon slaying stories — the Spanish
'Knights of the Fish'[26]— a mirror was used in a
more matter-of-fact way to cause a dragon to fight
against itself. As examples of the divining mirror
we have the magic mirror used by the wicked Queen
in 'Snow-White' and the magic mirror in the tale
of 'Friar Bacon and Friar Bungay'.[27]

If we turn from metals to clothes we shall find
hats nearly as important as crowns, the wizard's
hat, the cap of darkness, Jack's cap of wisdom,
the red cap by means of which fairies and witches
could levitate themselves. Cloaks are equally
important, from Elijah's mantle which descended to
Elisha, to cloaks of darkness and the magician's
cloak decorated with symbols of power, pentacles
and moons and runic scribbles. Shoes are symbols
of swiftness in their ordinary form, and when they
are heightened by magic they become the winged

sandals of Hermes or shoes of swiftness given to
Jack by the befuddled giant, or the seven league
boots stolen by Hop O' my Thumb. They are also
symbols of personality, like Cinderella's glass
slippers or the slipper into which Rashie-Coat's[28]
rival tried to crush her clumsy feet, so that the
bird sang as they passed:

'Nippit fit and clippit fit
Ahint the king's son rides,
But bonny fit and pretty fit
Ahint the caudron hides',—

The envious rivals in these stories are people who
literally tried 'to step into other men's shoes'
or were 'too big for their boots'.

So much for the work of men's hands; though
there is much more that could be said about arte-
facts, particularly of spinning and weaving and of
smithy work.

It is time to go on to nature. We can perhaps
neglect the symbolism of Astrology, which was an
art for the learned and did not make much mark on
fairy tales. But the sun and all the things associated with the sun are present in one form or
another in many fairy stories, though less ex-
plicitly than in most in 'The Bright Sun Brings it
to Light' (Grimm 115). Everywhere the sun symbolises fertility and life. Evil spirits are driven
away by sunrise, hauntings cease, to go widdershins is to put oneself into the power of darkness
and of evil spirits, cockcrow is potent for good.

The moon is more ambivalent. The full moon is
the time when fairies are abroad and powerful, but
the light of the moon is welcomed with gratitude.
'The Dead Moon'[29] recorded by Mrs Balfour is a
Fenland fable in which the moon is an entirely
beneficent character driving away the evil bogles
and malevolent ghosts which infest the fens and
making the paths safe for the fenmen. One night,
going down to judge of the evil done by the bogles,

151

she is trapped and burns down into the bog, and for over a month no moon shines and all evil things spread abroad. At length the fenmen take counsel from a wise woman, and by her advice find the buried moon and release her again, so that she shines once more in the heavens and the evil things are driven back. Grimm 175, 'The Moon', gives a more humorous and matter-of-fact fable about the origin of the moon, but here too the moon is entirely beneficent.

In days gone by there was a land where the nights were always dark, and the sky spread over it like a black cloth, for there the moon never rose, and no star shone in the gloom. At the creation of the world, the light at night had been sufficient. Three young fellows once went out of this country on a travelling expedition, and arrived in another kingdom, where, in the evening when the sun had disappeared behind the mountains, a shining globe was placed on an oak-tree, which shed a soft light far and wide. By means of this, everything could very well be seen and distinguished, even though it was not so brilliant as the sun. The travellers stopped and asked a countryman who was driving past with his cart, what kind of light that was. 'That is the moon,' answered he; 'our mayor bought it for three talers, and fastened it to the oak-tree. He has to pour oil into it daily, and to keep it clean, so that it may always burn clearly. He receives a taler a week from us for doing it.'

When the countryman had driven away, one of them said: 'We could make some use of this lamp, we have an oak-tree at home, which is just as big as this, and we could hang it on that. What a pleasure it would be not to have to feel about at night in the darkness!' 'I'll tell you what we'll do,' said the second; 'we will fetch a cart and horses and carry away the moon. The

people here may buy themselves another.' 'I'm a
good climber,' said the third, 'I will bring it
down.' The fourth brought a cart and horses, and
the third climbed the tree, bored a hole in the
moon, passed a rope through it, and let it down.
When the shining ball lay in the cart, they
covered it over with a cloth, that no one might
observe the theft. They conveyed it safely into
their own country, and placed it on a high oak.
Old and young rejoiced, when the new lamp let
its light shine over the whole land, and bed-
rooms and sitting-rooms were filled with it. The
dwarfs came forth from their caves in the rocks,
and the tiny elves in their little red coats
danced in rings on the meadows.

The four took care that the moon was provided
with oil, cleaned the wick, and received their
weekly taler, but they became old men, and when
one of them grew ill, and saw that he was about
to die, he appointed that one quarter of the
moon, should, as his property, be laid in the
grave with him. When he died, the mayor climbed
up the tree, and cut off a quarter with the
hedge-cutters, and this was placed in his coffin.
The light of the moon decreased, but still not
visibly. When the second died, the second
quarter was buried with him, and the light dim-
inished. It grew weaker still after the death of
the third, who likewise took his part of it away
with him; and when the fourth was borne to his
grave, the old state of darkness recommenced,
and whenever the people went out at night without their lanterns they knocked their heads
together in collision.

When, however, the pieces of the moon had united
themselves together again in the world below,
where darkness had always prevailed, it came to
pass that the dead became restless and awoke
from their sleep. They were astonished when they

were able to see again; the moonlight was quite sufficient for them, for their eyes had become so weak that they could not have borne the brilliance of the sun. They rose up and were merry, and fell into their former ways of living. Some of them went to the play and to dance, others hastened to the public-houses, where they asked for wine, got drunk, brawled, quarrelled, and at last took up cudgels, and belaboured each other. The noise became greater and greater, and at last reached even to heaven.

Saint Peter, who guards the gate of heaven, thought the lower world had broken out in revolt and gathered together the heavenly hosts, which were employed to drive back the Evil One when he and his associates storm the abode of the blessed. As these, however, did not come, he got on his horse and rode through the gate of heaven, down into the world below. There he reduced the dead to subjection, bade them lie down in their graves again, took the moon away with him, and hung it up in heaven.

The wind is often personified in fairy tales, as the West Wind in the Scandinavian 'Soria Moria Castle',[30] or the North Wind which repays Hans for the meal he has blown away. But water is perhaps the most potent natural force in fairy tales. Death and Division is symbolised by rivers. We have healing streams, such as that in 'The King's Son Who Feared Nothing', or enchanted streams that transform those who drink from them, as in 'Brother and Sister', Grimm No.11. Wells are often the gates to an underwater country or contain the Water of Life. Grimm 97 is devoted to the Quest for the Water of Life from the Fountain of Lions. Mysterious heads that bless or curse can rise out of wells. These trunkless heads remind us of those decapitated heads, like the Head of Bron[31] which seemed more potent after death than his whole body

154

had been in life and gave counsel, prosperity and happiness wherever it was carried. So a dried bone which symbolised the life of the whole man had power to speak or sing and demand vengeance on its murderer, as in the Ballad of Binnorie, Child 29 or Grimm's 'Singing Bone', No.29. Even the head of an animal may have special power like the head of the talking horse, Falada, in Grimm's 'Goosegirl', No.81, that spoke from the wall where it was hanging.

Time does not serve me to tell of magical precious stones or of symbolic trees and plants in fairy tales, nor of the many magical animals: we have come across a lion in Grimm 545, and a lion as the primate among the animals merits special attention; but we have horses, deer, foxes, dogs, cats and birds, some of them enchanted humans, but many of them magical in their own right. A book might be written on the subject, and I have tried to keep you for less than an hour so as to allow time for contributions from those more competent than myself to deal with the philosophic aspect of the subject. I must apologise if I have sometimes seemed to gallop over the ground and sometimes to loiter, but I judged that a steady hand-gallop would be wearisome to us all.

NOTES

1. *Religious Symbols and Indian Thought*

   F.R.Allchin

ABBREVIATIONS

AU *Aitareya Upaniṣad*
AV *Atharvaveda*
BAU *Brihadāraṇyaka Upaniṣad*
BG *Bhagavadgītā*
KU *Kaṭha Upaniṣad*
RCM *Rāmacaritamānasa*
RV *Rigveda*
SB *Śatapatha Brāhmaṇa*
SU *Śvetāśvatara Upaniṣad*
TU *Taittirīya Upaniṣad*
VS *Vājasaneyi Saṃhitā*

1 The principal references in Tillich's writings
  are: 'The religious symbol', *J.Liberal Religion*
  2(1940), pp.15-19; 'Theology and symbolism' in
  F.E.Johnson, ed. *Religious Symbolism*, London
  (1955), pp.107-16; 'Religious symbols and our
  knowledge of God' *The Christian Scholar* 38
  (1955), pp.189-90; *Dynamics of Faith*, London
  (1957), pp.41-54. Other relevant works are W.L.
  Rowe, *Religious Symbols and God, a philosophical
  study of Tillich's theology*, Chicago (1968);
  G.L.Maclean, 'Symbol and analogy: Tillich and
  Thomas', in T.F.O'Meara, ed. *Paul Tillich and
  Catholic Thought*, New York (1969); G.Tavard,
  'Christology as Symbol' in T.F.O'Meara, *ibid.*
  pp.269-88.

2 Tillich in F.E.Johnson, ed. *op.cit.* 1955, pp.108-
  11.

3 *ibid.* pp.113-5; *Theology and Culture*, New York
  (1959), pp.61-3.

4 *SB* XI.2.3.

5 *BAU* 1.6.

6 *RCM* Bāla kāṇḍa I.12, 1-3.

7 *ibid.* I.18.1-19.4.

8 *ibid.* I.20.1-4.

9 *ibid.* I.22.1-23.

10 *RV* I.164.

11 An approach to the broader aspects of the symbolism of the wheel in Indian thought has been made by Vāsudeva Śaraṇa Agrāwāl, *Chakra-Dhvaja the wheel-flag of India*, Banāras (1964).

12 F.Edgerton, *The Beginnings of Indian Philosophy*, London (1964), p.19. For discussion of the many aspects of Vāc in the *RV*, see A.Bergaigne, *La Religion Védique d'après les hymns du Rigveda*, Paris (1878), I.277-311.

13 *RV* X.71.4.

14 *RV* X.115.

15 *RV* I.164.34-5, 45.

16 *RV* I.1. For a full exposition of Agni and his position in the sacrifice, see Bergaigne, *op. cit.*I.11-149.

17 'Gāyatrī mantra and the beginnings of Indian theology' in press.

18 *RV* I.115.1.

19 *RV* X.114.5., I.164.46.

20 *VS* 40.17.

21 *KU* 1, 2.16-18.

22 *TU*.1.8.

23 *BG* VII.8.

24 *BG* VIII.13.

25 *Satyārtha Prakāś*, Ajmer (1971), 9.

26 Bergaigne, *op.cit.* I. Introduction.

27 A.B.Keith, *Religion and Philosophy of the Vedas and Upaniṣads*, I.pp.252 ff.

28 *RV* X.90. Keith, *op.cit.* pp.437-8; R.C.Zaehner, *Hinduism*, p.44.

29 *RV* I.164.34-35.

30 Keith, *op.cit.* 454.

31 *Īśa U*.2; *Muṇḍaka U.* I.ii.

32 *BG* II.42-4.

33 *BG* III.10-14.

34 *BG* IV.17.

35 *BG* IV.32.

36 Bergaigne, *op.cit.* I. pp.127-32.

37 M.Dhavamony, *Love of God according to the Śaiva Siddhānta*, Oxford (1971), pp.63-67; Sabapathy Kulandran, *Grace, a comparative study of the doctrine in Christianity and Hinduism*, London (1964).

38 *TU* I.11.

39 *AU*, *Śānti mantra*.

40 *Kabīr Granthāvalī*, ed. S.S.Dās. Banāras (1957). I.1.3.

41 *ibid.* I.1.6.

42 *Saral Sāhitya*, ed. K.S.Misra. Indore (n.d.). p.1.

43 S.S.Dās, *op.cit.*I.1.26.

44 *ibid.* I.1.2.

45 Jñānadeva, *Amṛtānubhava*, Poona (1956), II.6.

46 *ibid.* II.26.

47 *ibid.* II.28.

48 *ibid,* II.43.

49 *ibid.* II.61.

50 W.H.Macleod, *Guru Nānak and the Sikh Religion*, Oxford (1968), pp.196-9

51 *Śūnyasampadane*, Dharwar (1965), I.29-30.

52 *ibid.* I.30-35.

53 *ibid.* I.40.

54 *ibid.* I.42-3.

55 *BG* IV.34.

56 *BG* X.9.

57 *Jñāneśvarī*, X.119-127.

58 *Vinayapatrikā* 57.

59 *RCM* I.2.

60 *Śūnyapampādane* VII.2-3.

61 *ibid.* IV.42-3.

62 K.C.Varadachari, *Ālvārs of South India*, Bombay (1966) p.101; Tukārām, Abhanga 320.

63 *Viṣṇudharmottara Purāṇa*, 103-8.

64 *BG* XII.1-5.

65 *VS* XVI.

66 J.Gonda has recently published exhaustive *Notes on names and the name of God in ancient India*, Amsterdam (1970).

67 In the opening credal statement of the Jāpjī, Ādigranth, p.1.

68 *SU* VI.9.

69 *KU* VI.8.

70 *Anuśāsana Parva*, 14.231-3.

71 It is not clear when this system of thirty-six *tattvas* first developed. It seems indubitable that it was later than the twenty-five or six *tattvas* of the Sānkhya system.

72 *Sauptika Parva*, 17-18.

73 This topic has been developed by W.D.O'Flaherty, *Asceticism and Eroticism in the mythology of Śiva*, Oxford (1973).

74 *Linga Purāṇa* III.1, 2.

75 *ibid.* III 1, 4.

76 S.Nandimath, *Handbook of Vīraśaivism*, Dharwar (1942) pp.50-64.

77 See my 'The attaining of the Void', *Religious Studies* 7, (1971) pp.353-4.

78 Quoted by H.Thipperudra Swamy, *The Vīraśaiva saints — a study*, Mysore (1968) p.203.

79 *ibid.* pp.204-5.

80 *Vacanás of Basavaṇṇa*, ed. H.Deveerappa, Siri-gere (1967), no.950.

81 *ibid.* no.949.

82 For a development of related ideas on time in Indian thought see M.Eliade, *Images and Symbols*, London (1961), ch.II, particularly pp.67-71.

2. The World to Come

Michael Loewe

1 I.e., the *Ch'u Tz'u*; see D.Hawkes, *Ch'u Tz'u,
The Songs of the South* (Clarendon Press, 1959).

2 I am hoping to publish a fuller interpretation
and description of the painting in due course.
Colour reproductions of the painting are available in *Hsi Han po hua* (Peking, 1972).

3. The Old English Runic Paternoster

Eric J.Sharpe

1 G.Ebeling, *The Lord's Prayer in Today's World*
(E.T. London 1966), 62.

2 J.M.Kemble, *The Dialogue of Salomon and Saturnus*
(London 1848), 134 ff.

3 This is probably the most difficult question of
all to settle, since in other versions, Solomon's
partner is Marcolf, who seems to be identified
with Mercurius, and therefore would represent
Odin. On this subject, see Kemble's introduction,
and R.J.Menner, *The Poetical Dialogues of
Solomon and Saturn* (New York and London 1941),
31 ff.

4 The unusual expression 'palm-twigged' (*gepalm-
twigede*) may, as Menner suggests, have a ritual
setting, being due ultimately to a memory on the
poet's part of an actual tablet of the Pater
Noster ornamented with palm-branches. *Op.cit.*,
43 ff.

5 The relevant letters, here capitalised in the
context of the Latin prayer, are as follows:

PATER NOS(ter), QUI (es) (in) C(ae)L(is):
(sancti)F(icetur) (no)M(en) (tuum).
(A)D(veniat) (re)G(num) (tuum).
(Fiat voluntas tua, sicut in caelo, et in
                                    terra.)
(Panem nostrum) (quotidianum) (da) (no)B(is)
                                    H(odie).

6 Kemble, *op.cit.*, 139-141.

7 He speaks of 'The fantastic superstition and childish literalism of Poem I...' in *op.cit.*, p.6. And further: '...the pleasant fiction of the dialogue in which Solomon instructs Saturn seems to become imperceptibly the instruction of his ignorant contemporaries by the author.' *Ibid.*, 36.

8 A possible exception would be the clause 'Sed libra nos a malo' ('But deliver us from evil').

9 *Hávamál*, 139 ff.

10 Menner, *op.cit.*, 49: 'Thus, though the runic letters in Poem I are simply those of the Christian prayer, their very appearance as personified conquerors of demons represents the last vestige of an ancient pagan Germanic tradition...'

11 Cf. Sharpe, 'Salvation, Germanic and Christian', in Sharpe and Hinnells (eds.), *Man and his Salvation: Studies in Memory of S.G.F.Brandon* (Manchester 1973), 243 ff.

12 R.I.Page, 'Runes and Non-Runes', in Pearsall and Waldron (eds.), *Medieval Literature and Civilization* (London 1969), 28. For a review of older attitudes, see G.Jaffé, *Geschichte der Runenforschung* (Berlin/Leipzig 1937).

13 Quoted by Page, *op.cit.*, 51.

14 R.W.V.Elliott, *Runes: An Introduction* (Manchester 1963), 11.

15 *Ibid.*, 11 f.

16 S.B.F.Jansson, *Runinskrifter i Sverige* (Stockholm 1963), 67 f., cf. *idem*, 'De foro dristigt', in *STF:s årsskrift* (1949), 101 ff.

17 B.af Klintberg, *Svenska trollformler* (Stockholm 1965), 9.

18 *Ibid.*, 22.

19 Cf. J.K.Hewison, *The Runic Roods of Ruthwell and Bewcastle* (Glasgow 1914), passim.

20 B.Dickins (ed.), *Runic and Heroic Poems of the Old Teutonic Peoples* (Cambridge 1915).

21 *Ibid.*, 17.

22 K.Schneider, *Die germanische Runennamen: Versuch einer Gesamtdeutung* (Meisenheim 1956), 558 ff.

23 Cf. Å.V.Ström, 'Scandinavian Belief in Fate', in Ringgren (ed.), *Fatalistic Beliefs* (Stockholm 1967), 63 ff.

24 S.Agrell, *Lapptrummor och runmagi* (Lund 1934), pp.49 ff.

25 The Tyr rune was cut on the Loveden Hill cremation urns (Lincolnshire), and a 6th-century sword pommel from Faversham, Kent, has an engraved pattern which may be the same rune. *Sigrdrífumál* says: 'If you want victory, learn victory runes and cut them on your sword hilt, ...and name Týr twice.' Page, *Life in Anglo-Saxon England* (London 1970), 28 f.

26 Dickins, *op.cit.*, 15.

27 *Ibid.*, 25.

28 *Ibid.*, 29.

29 Schneider, *loc.cit.*

30 Å.Fredsjö and others, *Hallristningar i Sverige* (Stockholm 1969), 33, 96, 123.

31 *Bhagavad Gītā* I:12-19.

32 Agrell, *op.cit.*, 25 f.

33 P.G.Foote, in *Medieval Literature and Civilization*, ed. Pearsall and Waldron (London 1969), 135.

34 Menner, *op.cit.*, 35. Otherwise, one's con- fidence in the judgment of this author is not increased by observing such a comment as that on p.6: 'The fantastic superstition and child- ish literalism of Poem I (that in which the Runic section is found) give way in Poem II to cryptic questions on Oriental legend...' It is a matter of some importance, when faced with a text such as this, that we should *not* give way to such facile value judgments. Unless we attempt to read it in the same spirit in which it was written, we shall never begin to under- stand it, or to unravel its religious and psychological complexities.

35 See e.g. H.Fuchs, 'Die Herkunft der Sator- formel', in *Schweiz. Archiv f. Volkskunde* 47 (1951).

4. *Icons as Symbols of Power*

   Venetia Newall

ABBOT, G.F., *The Tale of a Tour in Macedonia* (London, 1903).

ALPATOW, Michael, *Altrussische Ikononmalerei* (Dresden, 1958).

AMEISENOWA, Zofia, 'Animal-Headed Gods, Evangelists, Saints and Righteous Men', *Journal of the Warburg and Courtauld Institutes* (London, 1949), XII.

ATTWATER, Donald, *A Dictionary of Mary* (London, 1957).

ATTWATER, Donald, *Saints of the East* (London, 1963).

ATTWATER, Donald, *The Penguin Dictionary of Saints* (London, 1965).

BASSILI, W.F., *Sinai and the Monastery of St Catherine* (Cairo, 1962).

BAULIER, Francis, and BEGUIGNON, Yves, *Greece* (Paris, 1955).

BENZ, Ernst, *The Eastern Orthodox Church: Its Thought and Life* (Chicago, 1963).

BIHALJI-MERIN, Oto, 'Naive Art in Yugoslavia', *Jugoslavija* (Belgrade, 1959), XVII.

BILLINGTON, J.H., *The Icon and the Axe* (New York, 1966).

BOURDEAUX, Michael, *Opium of the People* (London, 1965).

BRÉHIER, Louis, *L'Art Chrétien: Son Dévelopment Iconographique* (Paris, 1928).

BROWN, Theo, 'Some Examples of Post Reformation Folklore in Devon', *Folklore* (London, June 1961), LXXII.

BUNT, Cyril, *Russian Art: From Scythes to Soviets* (London, 1946).

CHAPMAN, Olive, *Across Cyprus* (London, 1945).

CHIERICHETTI, Sandro, *Ravenna* (Milan, 1960).

COMAMESCU, Petru, *Voroneţ* (Bucharest, 1959).

ĆOROVIĆ-LJUBANOVIĆ, Mirjana, 'Ohrid Icons',
  Jugoslavija (Belgrade, 1952), V.
DALE-GREEN, Patricia, *Dog* (London, 1966).
DAWKINS, R.M., *The Monks of Athos* (London, 1936).
DOURNOVO, Lydia, *Armenian Miniatures* (London, 1961).
ENGELHARDT, Walter, *Klinzy: Bildnis einer russi-
  schen Stadt nach ihrer Befreiung vom Bolschweis-
  mus* (Berlin, 1943).
FARBMAN, Michael, ed., *Masterpieces of Russian
  Painting* (London, 1930).
FEDOTOV, G.P., *The Russian Religious Mind* (Cam-
  bridge, Mass., 1946), 2 vols.
FERGUSON, George, *Signs and Symbols in Christian
  Art* (Oxford, 1961).
FLETCHER, W.C., *A Study in Survival: The Church in
  Russia 1927-43* (London, 1965).
FORTE, John, ed., *Corfu: Venus of the Isles*
  (Clacton-on-Sea, 1963).
FORTESCUE, Adrian, *The Uniate Eastern Churches*
  (New York, 1923).
FRENCH, R.M., *Icons and How They Were Made* (Lon-
  don, 1936).
FRENCH, R.M., *The Eastern Orthodox Church* (London,
  1951).
GEORGES, Robert A., 'The Greeks of Tarpon Springs:
  An American Folk Group', *Southern Folklore
  Quarterly* (June, 1965), XXIX.
GERHARD, H.P., *The World of Icons* (London, 1971).
GOGOL, Nikolai, *Dead Souls* (London, 1957).
GRABAR, André, *Byzantine Painting: Historical and
  Critical Study* (New York, 1953).
GRABAR, André, and OPRESCU, Georges, *Rumania —
  Painted Churches of Moldavia* (New York, 1962).
GROVE, H.M., *Moscow* (London, 1912).
GRUNWALD, Constantin de, *Saints of Russia* (London,
  1960).
GUNNIS, Rupert, *Historic Cyprus* (London, 1936).
HACKETT, J., *A History of the Orthodox Church of*

Cyprus (London, 1901).

HAMILTON, George H., *The Art and Architecture of Russia* (Harmondsworth, 1954).

HAMILTON, Mary, *Greek Saints and their Festivals* (Edinburgh, 1910).

HARE, Richard, *The Art and Artists of Russia* (London, 1965).

HASLER, J., *The Making of Russia* (London, 1969).

HASTINGS, James, ed., *Encyclopaedia of Religion and Ethics* (Edinburgh, 1910), III.

HECKER, Julius, *Religion and Communism* (London, 1933).

HOLE, Christina, *Saints in Folklore* (London, 1965).

HOWELL SMITH, A.D., *Thou Art Peter* (London, 1950).

HOWE, Sonia, *Some Russian Heroes, Saints and Sinners* (London, 1916).

IDELSOHN, Abraham Z., *The Ceremonies of Judaism* (New York, 1930).

IRIMIE, Cornel, and FOCŞA, Marcela, *Romanian Icons Painted on Glass* (Bucharest, 1969).

IRIMIE, Cornel, and FOCŞA, Marcela, *Icoane pe Sticlă* (Bucharest, 1971).

ISWOLSKY, Helene, *Christ in Russia* (Kingswood, 1960).

KOLARZ, Walter, *Religion in the Soviet Union* (London, 1961).

KONDAKOV, N.P., *The Russian Icon* (Oxford, 1927).

LASAREFF, Victor, and DEMUS, Otto, *USSR: Early Russian Icons* (New York, 1958).

LAWSON, John C., *Modern Greek Folklore and Ancient Greek Religion* (New York, 1964).

LOSSKY, Vladimir, *The Mystical Theology of the Eastern Church* (London, 1957).

LUCIE-SMITH, Edward, 'The True Function of Icons', *The Times* (December 7, 1965).

MACDERMOTT, Marcia, *A History of Bulgaria 1393-1885* (London, 1962).

MAKHAIRAS, Leontios, *Recital Concerning the Sweet*

Land of Cyprus entitled 'Chronicle' (Oxford, 1932), 2 vols.

MANDEL, Benjamin, The Church and State Under Communism (Washington, 1965).

MANDIĆ, Svetislav, 'The Delicate Lines of an Old Art', Jugoslavija (Belgrade, 1958), XV.

MEER, F.Van Der, and MOHRMANN, Christine, Atlas of the Early Christian World (London, 1958).

MEGAS, George A., Greek Calendar Customs (Athens, 1963).

MEYENDORFF, J., The Orthodox Church (London, 1962).

MULOCK, Cawthra, and LANGDON, Martin T., The Icons of Yuhanna and Ibrahim the Scribe (London, 1946).

MURATOV, P.R., Les Icones Russes (Paris, 1927).

MUSICESCU, Maria Ana, Voroneţ (Bucharest, 1969).

NICOLESCU, Corina, Icônes Roumaines (Bucharest, 1971).

OBSERVER, The, 'Powers of Icons' (London, March 8. 1964); (London, March 4.1973).

ONASCH, Konrad, Icons (London, 1963).

OUSPENSKY, Leonid, and LOSSKY, Vladimir, The Meaning of Icons (Boston, Mass., 1952).

PAGLIA, J., Rome and Environs (Rome, N.D.).

PROTITCH, André, Guide à Travers Bulgaria: Archéologie, Histoire, Art (Sofia, 1923).

READ, Herbert, Icon and Idea (London, 1955).

RICCARDI, Balilla, Madre del Buon Consiglio (Rome, May, 1960) LXIII; 4-5.

RICE, David Talbot, The Icons of Cyprus (London, 1937).

RICE, David Talbot, The Beginnings of Russian Icon Painting (Oxford, 1938).

RICE, Tamara Talbot, A Concise History of Russian Art (London, 1963).

RICE, Tamara Talbot, Russian Icons (London, 1963).

RODD, Rennell, The Customs and Lore of Modern Greece (Chicago, 1892).

ROUX, Jeanne and Georges, Greece (London, 1958).

SANDERS, Irwin T., *Balkan Village* (Lexington, Kentucky, 1949).

SAVA, George, *One Russian's Story* (London, 1970).

SCHUG-WILLE, Christa, *Art of the Byzantine World* (New York, 1969).

SOKOLOV, Y.M., *Russian Folklore* (New York, 1950).

SPICER, Dorothy, *The Book of Festivals* (New York, 1937).

SPINKA, Matthew, *The Church in Soviet Russia* (New York, 1956).

STEWART, Cecil, *Serbian Legacy* (London, 1959).

SVIRINE, A., *La Peinture de l'Ancienne Russie* (Moscow, 1958).

TIMES, The, 'Critical Condition of King Paul' (March 4.1964).

TOLSTOY, Leo, *War and Peace* (Oxford, 1942).

TOZER, Henry F., *Researches in the Highlands of Turkey* (London, 1869), I.

TWEEDY, Mark, *Wheat Among the Tares* (Mirfield, 1959).

VALENTIN, Jacques, *The Monks of Athos* (London, 1960).

WALLACE, Robert, *The Rise of Russia* (Netherlands, 1967).

WARE, Timothy, *The Orthodox Church* (Harmondsworth, 1963).

WILD, Doris, *Holy Icons* (Berne, 1961).

ZAEHNER, R.C., *Concise Encyclopaedia of Living Faiths* (London, 1964).

ZATKO, James J., *Descent into Darkness* (Notre Dame, Indiana, 1965).

ZERNOV, Nicholas, *Eastern Christendom* (London, 1961).

5. *Quest for The Green Man*

  K.H.Basford

1 C.J.P.Cave, 'The Roof Bosses in Ely Cathedral', *Proceedings and Communications, Cambridge Antiquarian Society*, 32 (1932) 33-46.

2 Lady Raglan, 'The "Green Man" in Church Architecture', *Folklore*, 50 (1939) 45-57.

3 Fritz Saxl, *A Heritage of Images* (Penguin Books, 1970) 14.

4 K.H.Basford, 'The Foliate Head', letter to *Folklore* 79 (1968) 59-61.

5 Max Wegner, 'Blattmasken', *Das siebente Jahrsehnt. Festschrift zum 70. Geburtstag von Adolph Goldschmidt* (Berlin, 1935) 43-50; Harald Keller, 'Blattmaske', *Reallexikon zur deutschen Kunstgeschichte*, vol.2 (Stuttgart, 1948) 867-874.

6 J.M.C.Toynbee and J.B.Ward Perkins, 'Peopled Scrolls: A Hellenistic Motif in Imperial Art', *Papers of the British School in Rome*, 18 (1950) 1-43.

7 Nelson Glueck, *Deities and Dolphins. The Story of the Naboteans* (London, 1964) 335-6.

8 J.M.C.Toynbee, *Art in Britain Under the Romans* (London, 1964) pp.134 ff.

9 *Ibid.* pp.308 ff; plate LXXI; *Art in Roman Britain* (London, 1962) pp.163-4

10 Wilhelm von Massow, *Die Grabmäler von Neumagen* (Berlin und Leipzig, 1932).

11 Keller, (note 5 above).

12 von Massow, (note 10 above).

13 J.M.C.Toynbee (personal communication).

14 O.Navarre, 'Persona', *Dictionaire des Antiqui-
tés greques et romaines* (Daremberg, Saglio,
Pottier, 1877) 4, 406.

15 J.N.von Wilmowsky, *Der Dom zu Trier* (Trier,
1874).

16 Theodor Konrad Kempf, 'Untersuchungen und
Beobachtungen am Trierer Dom.1961-63', *Germania*
42 (1964) 126-41.

17 Erich Gose, 'Der Tempel am Herrenbrünnchen in
Trier', *Trierer Zeitschrift für Geschichte und
Kunst des Trierer Landes und seiner Nachbarge-
biete*, 30 (1967) 82-100.

18 Edith Mary Wightman, *Roman Trier and the
Treveri* (London, 1970) 111.

19 Edmond le Blant, *Les sarcophages chrétiens de
la Gaule* (Paris, 1886) p.85; H.Leclercq,
*Dictionnaire d'archéologie chrétienne et lit-
urgie* (Paris, 1939) 14, col.1315 and 1335.

20 Gustave Mendel, *Musée impériaux ottomans:
Catalogue des sculptures grecques, romaines et
byzantines* (1912-14) 2, 546-49.

21 *Patrologia Latina* (J.P.Migne, Paris, 1878-90)
112, col.1037.

22 Willibald Kirfel, *Die Dreiköpfige Gottheit*
(Bonn, 1948) 147 ff, 158 ff; R.Pettazzoni, 'The
Pagan origin of the three-headed representation
of the Christian Trinity', *Journal of the Warburg and Courtauld Institutes* 9 (1946), 135-151.

23 Herbert Schade, *Dämonen und Monstren* (Regens-
burg, 1962) 43.

24 Jean Adhémar, 'La Fontaine de Saint-Denis',

Revue Archéologique (1936) 224-32.

25 Richard H.L.Hamann-Maclean, 'Antikenstudium in der Kunst des Mittelalters', *Marburger Jahrbuch für Kunstwissenschaft* 15 (1949-50) 157-250.

26 *Miniature della Enciclopedia Medioevale di Rabano Mauro* (Ed. A.M.Amelli, Monte Cassino, 1896) Plate 1. (MS c.1023).

27 Hans R.Hahnloser, *Villard de Honnecourt* (Vienna, 1935) 25-6.

28 Nikolaus Pevsner, *The Leaves of Southwell* (King Penguin Books, 1945); A.C.Seward, 'The foliage, flowers and fruit of Southwell Chapter House', *Proceedings of the Cambridge Antiquarian Society* 35 (1933-34) 1-32.

29 Geoffrey Grigson, *Looking and Finding* (Carousel Books, 1971).

30 *Medieval English Verse* (trans. by Brian Stone, Penguin Books, 1964) no.29.

31 T.S.Eliot, *The Waste Land*, 19-20.

6. *Protective Symbols in the Home*
   Christina Hole

1 J.Aubrey, *Remaines of Gentilisme and Judaiisme, 1686-7* (ed. James Britten, 1881) 104.

2 George Ewart Evans, *The Pattern under the Plough*, 1966, 66-7.

3 Personal Informant.

4 D.Strömbäck, *The Conversion of Ireland* (Viking Society* 1975) 24.

5 S.O.Addy, *Household Tales and Traditional Remains*... 1895, 127.

6 E.Porter, *Cambridgeshire Customs and Folklore*, 1969, 181.

7 Personal Informant.

8 F.T.Elworthy, *The Evil Eye*, 1895.

9 G.Zammit-Maempel, 'The Evil Eye and Protective Cattle Horns in Malta', *Folklore* 79 (1968) 2-3.

10 G.Zammit-Maempel, *op.cit.* 4ff.

11 T.W.Bagshawe, 'A Stable Charm from Hertfordshire', *Folklore* 66 (1955) 416-17.

12 A.Sandkelf, 'Singing Flails', *F.F.Communications* 136 (1949) 36ff.

13 Evans (note 2 above) 198ff.

7. *Symbols in Fairy Tales*

Katharine M.Briggs

1 *Man and his Symbols*. Edited by Carl C.Jung and M-L von Franz. Doubleday 1964.

2 'Jack the Giant-Killer'. Given by Sidney Hartland in *English Fairy and Folk Tales*, Scott Publishing Library. Collated from various chapbooks printed in Newcastle (1711-1835).

3 *The Grateful Dead*. Gerould, G.H., F.L.S. 1908.

4 *Motif-Index*. Motif-Index of Folk Literature. 6 vols. Copenhagen 1956 (second edition).

5 'The Old Wives Tale'. *Works of George Peele* ed. by A.H.Bullen 1888, vol.1.

6 'The Barra Widow's Son'. *Popular Tales of the West Highlands*. J.F.Campbell vol.II London 1890 4 vols.

7 'The King of Ireland's Son'. *Beside the Fire*, Douglas Hyde. David Nutt 1890.

8 'The Travelling Companion'. *Hans Christian Andersen Fairy Tales* vol.II Edmund Ward, 1955 4 vols.

9 *Clavicula Solomonis*. Brit.Mus.MS 36, 674.

10 'The Three Little Men in the Wood'. Grimm No.13 *Grimm's Fairy Tales*. Routledge and Kegan Paul. London 1948.

11 'The King's Son Who Feared Nothing'. Grimm 121.

12 'Child Rowland'. Source *Illustrations of Northern Antiquities*. Jamieson, R. Edinburgh 1814. Retold *English Fairy Tales*. Jacobs, J. Nutt 1890.

13 Campbell, J.F. *Popular Tales of the West Highlands*, vol.II p.57 1890.

14 *The Great Chain of Being*, Lovejoy, A.O. Harvard University Press 1936.

15 Child, F.J. *English and Scottish Popular Ballads* no.39. Vol.I New York 1957.

16 Ursia, I. 'The Gallows and the Golden Ball', *Journal of American Folklore* vol.79.

17 Chambers, R. *Popular Rhymes of Scotland*, Edinburgh 1870.

18 Grimm, No.130.

19 Giraldus Cambrensis, *The Itinerary through Wales*, cap.8. Bohn Library.

20 Jacobs, J. *More English Fairy Tales*. From Bar-
   ing Gould's Appendix to the first edition of
   Henderson's *Folklore of the Northern Counties*
   (dialect modified).

21 'The Briery Bush', Cecil Sharp, Novello, Folk-
   songs for Schools.

22 William of Newburgh, *Chronica Rerum Anglicarum*,
   Bk.I cap.28. Printed 1719.

23 Aubrey, *The Natural History and Antiquities of
   the County of Surrey*. 1718-19. Vol.III p.368.

24 Child, 'Hind Horn', No.17 vol.I.

25 'St.Patrick's Purgatory'. Giraldus Cambrensis,
   The Conquest of Ireland. Cap.5. Bohn Library.

26 Andrew Lang, *The Brown Fairy Book*.

27 *The Famous Historie of Fryer Bacon*. Included in
   Early English Prose Romances. W.J.Thoms, n.d.
   Routledge.

28 R.Chambers. *Popular Rhymes of Scotland* pp.66-68.

29 Mrs Balfour, 'Legends of the Lincolnshire Cars'.
   Folk-Lore, vol.II.

30 Andrew Lang, *The Red Fairy Book*.

31 *The Mabinogion*. Translated by G. and T.Jones,
   Everyman Library. 'Branwen Daughter of Llyr'.

INDEX